WALKING THROUGH
THE LAKE
DISTRICT

Elmhow, Grisedale

WALKING THROUGH
THE LAKE DISTRICT

MICHAEL DUNN

DAVID & CHARLES
Newton Abbot   London   North Pomfret (Vt)

Illustrations by David Birchall
Maps by Chris Dunn

British Library Cataloguing in Publication Data

Dunn, Michael
　Walking through the Lake District
　1. Lake District (England) – Description and travel –
　Guide-books
　I. Title
　914.27′ 804858　　　DA670.L1

ISBN 0-7153-8443-0

Photoset by Typesetters (Birmingham) Ltd
and printed in Great Britain
by Billings, Worcester
for David & Charles (Publishers) Limited
Brunel House　Newton Abbot　Devon

Published in the United States of America
by David & Charles Inc
North Pomfret　Vermont 05053　USA

PREFACE

This book is a celebration of the unique qualities of one of Britain's most important recreational resources, but at the same time it attempts to be both informative and practical, and to act as a guide to twenty-five days of walking designed to explore the best features of the Lake District. It tries to combine familiar routes (Dow Crag and the Old Man of Coniston from the Walna Scar road, for example) with less hackneyed ascents (such as Scafell Pike via Pen and Rough Crag), and it mixes hard mountain walking with rather more gentle excursions in the dales.

It could not have been written without the considerable help of a number of people, and I am grateful to John Taylor for his bibliographical assistance, Gwyn and Rosie Jones for lending their emergency typewriter, Sue Hall for her good-humoured editing, and most of all to David Birchall for his evocative line drawings and Chris Dunn for her maps, advice and encouragement, and (with our daughter Katie) companionship on a number of the walks.

CONTENTS

The Walks and How to Complete Them Safely   9

The Lakeland Horseshoe   22

Back o' Skidda'   77

The Roman Way   100

The North-Western Fells   137

The Valley Route   152

The Hidden Valleys   182

The Heart of Lakeland   190

Bibliography   215

Index   219

To Katie

THE WALKS AND HOW TO COMPLETE THEM SAFELY

The Lake District is undoubtedly the ideal centre for a walking holiday. Not only is the scenery outstanding, but the footpaths are plentiful and well defined and there is an abundance of open access land; accommodation of all types is easy to find and, as an added bonus, there is a decent pint awaiting the walker in almost every dale. Yet despite a plethora of books covering just about every conceivable aspect of life in the Lake District, relatively few are specially relevant to the walker and fewer still include substantial walks combining visits to the tops of several fells in one day. This book aims to overcome this problem by introducing a series of comparatively long walks which between them provide the framework for an exploration of all the major dales and mountain systems in the Lake District, and an introduction to the remarkable complexity of scenery and history encompassed within this unique area.

The essence of the book is a collection of seven walks, varying in length from fifteen to eighty-eight miles and split into up to seven sections. There is an astonishing variety in the twenty-five days' walking, from a simple lowland stroll (albeit in magnificent scenery) covering a mere six miles to an arduous mountain expedition along a high-level ridge for sixteen miles – perhaps as far as many walkers would wish to travel in one day on the high fells. These introductory comments describe the walks very briefly, but more importantly include basic notes on the accommodation available at the overnight stops, the availability of public transport, especially at the start and finish of each walk, and a range of simple but crucial safety precautions which should be taken to reduce risks on the mountains.

It is important to emphasise that the precise itineraries need not be followed slavishly, for two reasons. First, there are

The Helvellyn range, Patterdale
and Ullswater

connections between most of the different walks at the overnight
points, so there is tremendous scope for the selection of
appropriate routes to satisfy individual interests and capabilities.
For example, a four-day trek through the Lake District from its
south-west to north-east borders could use the Valley Route
from Boot to Wasdale Head, the superb walk over Pillar and
High Stile which is followed by the Lakeland Horseshoe on the
way to Buttermere, the North-Western Fells route over
Grisedale Pike to Keswick and, finally, from Keswick or
Threlkeld, the magnificent ascent of the Halls Fell ridge of
Blencathra described as part of the Back o' Skidda' walk, which
finishes in Mungrisdale. Again, a two- or three-day tour based
on Ambleside could make use of the Valley Route between
nearby Grasmere and Patterdale, the seventh leg of the Lakeland
Horseshoe from Patterdale to Troutbeck, and part of the Roman
Way walk from Troutbeck back to Ambleside.

The advantage of these possible itineraries is that they afford
an opportunity to sample the very different character and
attractions of several different valleys in a relatively short
excursion. More restricted but still very feasible is the adaptation
of some of the given routes into one-day circular walks. Quite
apart from the Hidden Valleys walk, which already qualifies and
is highly recommended as an appetiser for the eastern Lake

District, a number of others can be devised. For example, a walk based on Wasdale Head could take the Heart of Lakeland route over Great Gable and Base Brown as far as Seatoller, then return over Honister and Moses' Trod on the Valley Route. And in Great Langdale a long one-day route – effectively the Langdale Horseshoe – could tackle the first stage of the Heart of Lakeland walk over Crinkle Crags and Bowfell, returning by way of Angle Tarn and the Langdale Pikes, over paths followed as part of the final stage of the Heart of Lakeland walk.

The second factor to be considered in choosing and following a route is the state of many of the most popular paths. Although it is over-reacting to suggest, as Harry Griffin has, that the Lake District is being 'kicked to death' by the trampling feet of too many walkers, there is undoubtedly a serious problem. The really well-known key routes do suffer appalling erosion. While the measures so far taken to combat the problem have only 'scratched the surface', the scratches of walker's boots have hollowed out tracks in some places to a depth of several feet! So the walks in this book avoid many of the worst places and, wherever possible, alternative routes are given. In addition, it will be obvious from a study of the detailed maps that other possibilities exist, and they should certainly be explored. They will spread the load, and they may very well lead to a quieter and more enjoyable walk.

The seven walks

The Lakeland Horseshoe, at eighty-eight miles the longest of the seven walks, begins in Coniston and after seven days arrives at Troutbeck, near Windermere. Both Coniston and Troutbeck are within easy reach of Ambleside, so to all intents and purposes this is a circular walk, albeit on a prodigious scale. The first day is spent on the Coniston Fells, climbing the craggiest, Dow Crag, and the highest, the Old Man of Coniston. Scafell Pike and Scafell, the highest of the English mountains, are the twin objectives of the second stage. The walk then heads for Pillar, Ennerdale and the splendid High Stile ridge, and on the

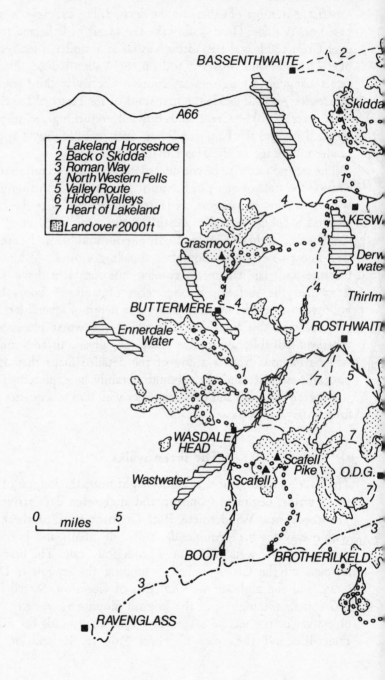

BASSENTHWAITE

A66

Skidda

1 Lakeland Horseshoe
2 Back o' Skidda'
3 Roman Way
4 North Western Fells
5 Valley Route
6 Hidden Valleys
7 Heart of Lakeland
▨ Land over 2000 ft

KESW

Grasmoor

Derw
wate

BUTTERMERE

ROSTHWAIT

Ennerdale
Water

Thirlm

WASDALE
HEAD

Scafell Pike

O.D.G.

Wastwater

Scafell

0   miles   5

BOOT

BROTHERILKELD

RAVENGLASS

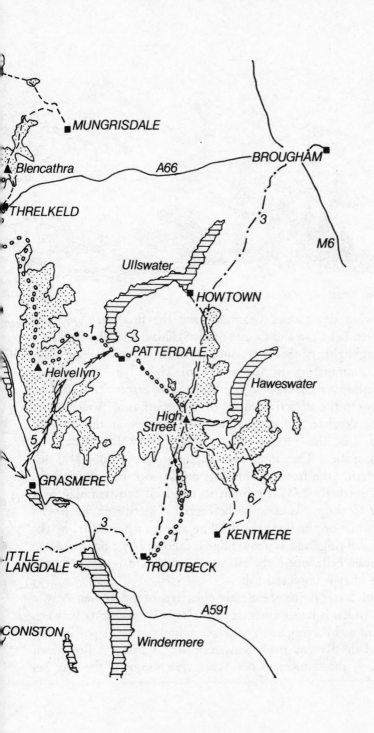

MUNGRISDALE

BROUGHAM

Blencathra   A66

THRELKELD

3

M6

Ullswater

HOWTOWN

1

PATTERDALE

Helvellyn

Haweswater

High
Street

5

6

GRASMERE

KENTMERE

3

LITTLE
LANGDALE   1

TROUTBECK

A591

CONISTON   Windermere

The head of Grisedale.

following day tackles Grasmoor and the fine array of peaks between Eel Crag and Causey Pike. Skiddaw and Blencathra are the highlights of the fifth stage, while the sixth is a long ridge walk culminating in the ascent of Helvellyn. Finally, the Horseshoe walk takes in Angle Tarn, High Street and Ill Bell on its way to the attractive village of Troutbeck near Windermere.

The desolate and usually deserted country at the Back o' Skidda' is the setting for a three-day walk centred on Mungrisdale. The first day explores the Caldbeck Fells, discovering the Iron Age hill fort on Carrock Fell, visiting the most northerly 2,000ft summit in Lakeland and tramping over Great Cockup. Skiddaw is the central objective of the second day, while on the third the thrilling ascent of Blencathra by the Halls Fell ridge and Narrow Edge is followed by a ridge walk to Bowscale Fell, where the attractive corrie tarn is reputedly the home of two immortal fish.

High Street is one of the early objectives of the Roman Way, a walk which is based on visits to the four Roman forts between Penrith and Ravenglass, and which follows as far as possible the line of the Roman roads between them. Starting at Brougham Castle – the remains of Brocavum are close by – the way lies upstream along the Eamont valley, then across the long High Street ridge, which takes its name from the Roman road, towards the fort of Galava at the head of Windermere. The route turns west here, towards Little Langdale, and climbs the passes of Wrynose and Hardknott to reach the superbly situated fort of Mediobogdum (Hardknott Castle) with its stupendous views over Eskdale. The way now lies along the Esk valley, past Boot and Muncaster Fell, to the sea at Glannaventa, just south of Ravenglass.

Familiar territory is at the heart of the two-day walk around the North-Western Fells. The walk from Keswick to the perfect miniature mountain of Catbells is extremely popular, though fewer walkers go on along the ridge to High Spy, Dale Head and eventually the village of Buttermere. The return to Keswick visits the summits of Grasmoor, Hopegill Head and, after a tremendous walk around the rim of Hobcarton Crag, Grisedale Pike before descending to the flood plains of the Newlands Beck and River Derwent.

The Valley Route deliberately avoids summits, yet on its way from Boot in Eskdale to the shores of Ullswater it climbs a series of high passes – most of them of great importance in the days of the packhorse trade – and between Wasdale Head and Honister it follows Moses' Trod, reputedly the route used by a whisky smuggler whose ruined hut can still be seen high on the craggy face of Great Gable. From Boot the route lies across Burnmoor to Wasdale Head; then by Moses' Trod to Honister and along the old toll road to Rosthwaite; next, along the Stonethwaite valley and over Greenup Edge to Far Easedale and Grasmere; and finally across Grisedale Hause, the high col separating the Helvellyn range from the Fairfield group of fells, on the way to Patterdale.

The Hidden Valleys walk, based on the village of Kentmere, introduces the comparatively unknown valleys of Kentmere and Longsleddale and at the same time visits the reservoir of Haweswater, the rocky eastern approaches to High Street and the fine mountains of Mardale Ill Bell and Harter Fell. A special attraction of this one-day walk is the chance to experience the perfect relationship between mountain and lake in these eastern fells. Two magnificent tarns, Blea Water and Small Water, and two very different reservoirs, Haweswater and Kentmere Reservoir, can be seen at close quarters during the course of the day.

The Old Dungeon Ghyll Hotel at the head of Great Langdale is both the start and finishing point for the Heart of Lakeland walk. This three-day excursion deliberately aims for the most spectacular scenery in the Lake District, and in some places opts for scrambling routes to the fell tops. The first stage climbs Pike of Blisco, then traverses the unique craggy ridge of Crinkle Crags before tackling Bowfell and Great End. The superb mountain of Great Gable is conquered next, by a direct route up Gavel Neese and over the rocks of White Napes. On the third day Glaramara, renowned for the wide views from its summit, and the Langdale Pikes are the principal targets, and there is the opportunity to finish with an exciting scrambling descent of Jack's Rake on Pavey Ark.

Accommodation

Altogether there are nineteen different towns and villages which form the starting or finishing point of a day's walk, and in such a popular holiday area as the Lake District it would be surprising if walkers were to find it difficult to secure a bed for the night in most of these places, except perhaps at the height of the season. The larger and more accessible settlements, such as Keswick and Coniston, are dominated by tourism and can offer a wide range and large amount of accommodation. In some of the remoter spots, however, the choice is much more limited and in these cases a few notes might be helpful.

At **Bassenthwaite** there are only a few possibilities in the village itself, but by the lake shore there are more hotels and guest houses. Taking **Boot** and **Brotherilkeld** together, this area of mid-Eskdale has a couple of inns and some farmhouse accommodation, but the total amount is fairly restricted. At **Howtown** there is an hotel and a few other possibilities, one of which is to take the lake steamer across Ullswater to Glenridding. **Mungrisdale** has a pub and guest house, together with bed and breakfast in some of the farms. Although **Threlkeld** is a large village, there is not a great deal of accommodation, although it is not far to Keswick (and there is a good bus service). At **Troutbeck** near Windermere there is a choice of inns or bed and breakfast. Finally, **Wasdale Head** has an excellent hotel but not much else; the fine hotels at Nether Wasdale are some four miles away at the far end of Wastwater.

Public transport

In common with the rest of rural Britain, the Lake District has seen drastic reductions in its public transport services, and some of the dales, such as Wasdale and Mardale, now have no conventional services at all. Other dales, notably Borrowdale and Great Langdale, have remarkably good bus services, and overall the picture is far from bleak, with some British Rail services, a narrow-gauge railway, ordinary bus services and Mountain Goat minibuses, and lake steamers on Coniston Water, Derwentwater, Ullswater and Windermere.

The crucial links in the system are the British Rail stations at Windermere, Penrith and (for Eskdale) Ravenglass, and the two long-distance bus routes, one calling at Windermere, Ambleside, Grasmere and Keswick, and the other running from Penrith to Keswick and Cockermouth. The relationship of these to the start and finish of the seven walks is as follows. The Lakeland Horseshoe begins in Coniston, served by buses from Ambleside, and ends at Troutbeck, which has bus connections on Tuesdays and Thursdays in high summer only to Ambleside, but in any case is only a short stroll from either Ambleside or Windermere. The Back o' Skidda' route begins and ends in Mungrisdale, which has a very infrequent bus service but is only two miles from the Keswick–Penrith road, where there are eight buses a day in each direction.

The Roman Way begins at Brougham, on the outskirts of Penrith, and ends at Ravenglass, on the Cumbrian west coast railway line. The North-Western Fells route begins and ends in

Keswick; if only one day's walking is required, to or from Buttermere, the Mountain Goat minibus service between the two places can be used for the return journey. The Valley Route starts from Boot, best reached by a delectable eight-mile ride on the Ravenglass & Eskdale narrow-gauge railway, and after four days reaches Patterdale, which has direct buses (six a day) along Ullswater to Pooley Bridge and Penrith. There is no public transport to Kentmere, start and finish of the Hidden Valleys walk; the nearest buses and trains are at Staveley, four miles down the valley. Finally, the Heart of Lakeland walk is based on the Old Dungeon Ghyll Hotel in Great Langdale, which is the terminus for a bus route from Ambleside.

Equipment and clothing

Incredible though it may seem, whole books have been written on this topic. Yet the basic essentials are self-evident: sufficient clothing to cope with the likely conditions and the bare minimum of equipment consistent with safety and comfort. A certain number of items qualify for inclusion in a comfortable day sack or rucksack. These include waterproof clothing (cagoule and overtrousers), spare sweaters, gloves, relevant maps and a compass, food and back-up emergency rations, basic first-aid equipment, a torch and whistle for safety reasons, and camera and lenses as required. The only other decisions involve normal outer clothing (some authorities have an aversion to jeans, which remain sodden longer after a downpour) and a choice of footwear. Here the guide should be comfort and reliability; there is certainly no need to choose expensive footwear for the sake of it, but a good strong pair of walking boots will prove a valuable asset. The temptation to follow the example of one recent writer who recommended wellies should be firmly resisted.

Route finding

The descriptions of the walks in this book are all accompanied by maps which show the line of the route, the mountains climbed,

Woodland path, near Derwent Water

the significant landmarks visited and the general lie of the land, with contours marked at 200ft intervals. They are based, with permission, on the Ordnance Survey maps but are intended as a general guide to a whole day's walking; for detailed route information the appropriate OS maps should be consulted. In the Lake District this means not the one-inch tourist map, which is not sufficiently detailed, but the four 1:25,000 scale Outdoor Leisure maps. These constitute a magnificent representation of the area, with the one reservation that many of the rights of way depicted in green are a dangerous nonsense, leading straight over crags or otherwise failing to show the real route taken by footpaths. Reference to the maps and detailed descriptions in this book should, however, minimise this problem. Maps are, of course, useless without the ability to read them accurately and to use them, in conjunction with a compass, in mist or other difficult conditions. It is essential to learn to recognise the symbols used on maps and to become familiar with the simple operations involved in using a compass correctly.

It is also important to select routes which are not only interesting but are within the capabilities of all members of the party, especially the weakest. A useful guide is the mileage to be covered, but this should be converted into time by using Naismith's formula (1 hour per 3 miles *plus* 1 hour for each 2,000ft ascended). For example, the Coniston Fells walk – the first leg of the Lakeland Horseshoe – should take, according to the formula, not 3 hours 40 minutes (11 miles at 3 miles per hour) but 5 hours 50 minutes (11 miles plus 4,300ft ascended). The calculation of height ascended should include not just the climb to the first fell top but also all the intermediate climbs from each col to each subsequent summit.

Weather

The general climate on the fell tops is very often severe, not only in winter. Driving rain, icy winds and mist can combine to create hazardous conditions even in the height of summer. The most important principle to grasp is the difference in temperature between the valley bottoms and the fell tops. There is no general rule, but walkers should expect a pleasantly mild day in the dales (say 17°C/63°F) to be equivalent to a distinctly cold day on the tops (say 6°C/43°F), with the additional likelihood on the tops of the fells of wind and rain. Waterproof clothing and extra supplies of warm clothing should therefore always be carried.

The temperatures quoted are actual summer examples from the forecasts issued by the Lake District Weather Service, which must rank as one of the most useful facilities available to the fell walker. The forecast, available every evening, covers the expected conditions for the following day, but also includes such crucial details as cloud base, dale and summit temperatures, and wind strength and direction. Like any other forecast it is fallible but, because it covers a comparatively small area, it is surprisingly accurate and it is certainly worth the cost of a local telephone call every evening. The number to ring is Windermere 5151.

Safety on the hills

Whatever the precautions taken, there is bound to be an element of risk involved in any walk in the mountains. No one can be certain that even a simple stroll will not end with a twisted ankle or an awkward descent in mist or even snow. The essence of safe fell walking is to take all possible precautions to reduce risks, yet to be prepared as far as possible for the unexpected situation and to have the knowledge and resources to cope with it.

Most of the factors involved have been dealt with in the preceding notes, but they bear repetition here. The walk should not be over-ambitious for any members of a party, bearing in mind that the speed and stamina of the weakest member should dictate the choice of route. With this in mind, it is worth noting that walking alone, whilst it can be immensely satisfying, should not be contemplated by the inexperienced or those unfamiliar with the terrain. All walkers should appreciate that there is anything but disgrace or failure in turning back if weather conditions worsen or a member of the group shows signs of illness or exhaustion.

Weather conditions are crucial to the success of most walks, especially on the fell tops. Mist need not be an insurmountable difficulty if the party knows how to navigate by map and compass, but driving winds, heavy rain and snow can be very dangerous. Walkers should be prepared for cold conditions on the tops, with adequate spare clothing at all times and, in winter, a survival bag and ice axe. Emergency food rations should always be carried, together with a basic first-aid kit (and the knowledge to use it). It is also prudent to take a torch and whistle in order to be able to give the recognised distress signal: six flashes or blasts repeated every minute.

Wherever possible it is wise to let someone know the expected time and place of arrival at the end of a walk – and to inform them of any changes – to avoid unnecessary worry and the possible call out of the Mountain Rescue service if the party fails to turn up as expected. Finally, since conditions can vary and necessitate a change of plans, it is worth getting to know the safe ways off the mountains and the best places to make for in an emergency; for example, Seatoller in upper Borrowdale has a late bus service to Keswick but the head of Ennerdale, only three miles away as the crow flies, is a long way from civilisation.

THE LAKELAND HORSESHOE

The Lakeland Horseshoe is an 88 mile circuit designed to include the summits of all four of the Lakeland Threethousanders and many of the other important fells, whilst visiting all of the main mountain systems in the Lake District. In a week's journey it provides a superb introduction to the fine mountain walking and breathtaking views for which the area is justly renowned. Inevitably, in visiting the major peaks, it treads well-known and heavily used paths at times. Wherever possible, however, alternative routes are offered and quieter routes of ascent are sought out to avoid the worst examples of the deeply worn tracks which scar the more popular fells. There are seven stages:

1. From Coniston to Brotherilkeld via Dow Crag, the Old Man of Coniston, Grey Friar and Hardknott Pass (11 miles/18km).
2. The ascent of the Scafell range from upper Eskdale, including Scafell Pike, Lord's Rake and Scafell (10 miles/16km).
3. Wasdale Head to Buttermere, via Steeple, Pillar, the Black Sail Pass and the High Stile ridge (13 miles/21km).
4. Grasmoor, Eel Crag, the ridge leading to Causey Pike and the edge of Derwentwater to Keswick (12 miles/19km).
5. The ascent of Skiddaw and Blencathra, ending at the village of Threlkeld (13 miles/21km).
6. The deserted settlement at Threlkeld Knotts, the Dodds and the Helvellyn ridge, Swirral Edge and Patterdale (16 miles/26km).
7. Via Angle Tarn, High Street and the Roman road, Ill Bell and the Garburn Pass to Troutbeck (13 miles/21km).

1 THE CONISTON FELLS
Coniston to Brotherilkeld (11 miles/18km)

The Lakeland Horseshoe begins in **Coniston**, a substantial village which now caters largely for tourists but was previously dependent for its prosperity on the surrounding fells (copper mines and slate quarries scar the face of the Old Man of Coniston) and, before that, was the centre of the small Norse kingdom of High Furness. The village, solidly built of the local blue and grey stone, presents a rather sombre façade even on the sunniest day. Nearby Coniston Water, narrow but straight, was the scene of Sir Donald Campbell's series of world water speed record attempts, the last of which, in January 1967, ended in tragedy. On the eastern shore, at Brantwood, was the home of John Ruskin, painter, art critic and social reformer, and the small Ruskin Museum in Coniston (housed in part of the Coniston Mechanics Institute and Literary Society) has some of his watercolours, drawings and geological specimens. Ruskin's grave, marked by a large grey-green cross from the quarries at nearby Tilberthwaite, is in the village churchyard.

Coniston copper mines lie on the eastern slopes of the Old Man of Coniston, and an interesting preparatory walk can be devised to take in the mines and Levers Water. The best approach is to follow Church Beck upstream, cross Miner's Bridge and take the rough track past a row of former miners' cottages. The mining of copper ores began around 1566, but the main period of exploitation started in 1758 and continued until the end of the eighteenth century. At first the copper ore was taken over Dunmail Raise to be smelted at Brigham near Keswick; later it was transported down Coniston Water and carried to Greenodd or Ulverston for shipment to Wales. The final phase of mining lasted from the 1830s to the 1860s, with as many as nine hundred men employed at times, but by now most of the better deposits had been worked out. The walk past the mine buildings, now a youth hostel, to Levers Water is unpleasantly stony underfoot in places but provides a fascinating insight into the past exploitation of Coppermines Valley.

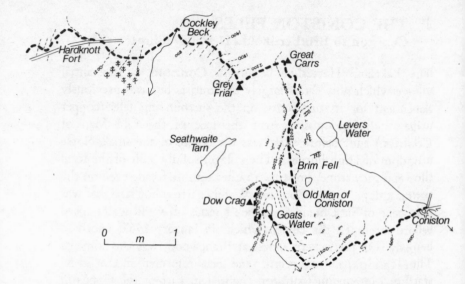

The route of the Lakeland Horseshoe leaves Coniston by crossing the main road at Church Beck Bridge and taking the lane leading west past the site of the former railway station. (Opened in 1859 to serve the copper mines, the Foxfield to Coniston branch line passed through outstandingly attractive scenery but was closed in 1957.) A narrow but well-surfaced minor road is now followed up a disconcertingly steep hill, round a sharp double bend and then more gently up to the fell gate, with the Old Man of Coniston looming ahead and to the right. The route lies straight on along a well-worn track, barely driveable yet likely to be busy with geologists' Land Rovers. This is the Walna Scar road, a prehistoric routeway from Coniston over the Walna Scar Pass – at 1,990ft the fifth highest in the Lake District – to Seathwaite in the Duddon valley.

Pass the steep track leading to Bursting Stone Quarry on the right and follow the Walna Scar road as it slowly rises across the southern flanks of the Old Man. To the left is Little Arrow Moor, with its Bronze Age burial mounds and small, overgrown stone circle. The next landmark used to be Boo Tarn, but the tarn seems to have virtually disappeared and all that is left is an unimpressive area of reed-choked marshy ground. There is usually more water in the hollows of the Walna Scar track. The tarn's name came from the Old Norse word 'booth' meaning hut, and there are some fragmentary remains nearby which may be foundations. There was once a rifle range here too (it was marked on older editions of the Ordnance Survey map), but that also has disappeared. A little further on is the spring marked on maps as Well in Crag.

The track now passes through a succession of rock gateways – interesting features in themselves and an enjoyable interlude after the trudge up the Walna Scar road – and, after the second of these, the path to Goats Water and Dow Crag ascends the fellside on the right. The path, rising steeply at first, is easily followed into The Cove, a vast tract of level wet ground below a hanging valley. The tarn is hidden during the boggy crossing of The Cove and a much more interesting subsequent episode tracing the winding path upwards on easy rocks, but as the scramble ends **Goats Water** springs into view, a dark jewel in a wild setting below the forbidding gullies and buttresses of Dow Crag. The wildness of the corrie is emphasised in thick mist, when the far shore of the tarn is invisible and the only evidence of the famous crag behind is the ghostly sound of rock climbers' karabiners glancing into the buttresses.

A first mist-free view of the sheer rock wall of Dow Crag is an awe-inspiring sight. Five tremendous buttresses plunge 600ft, almost vertically, from the summit ridge down to the boulder slope behind Goats Water. Between each pair of buttresses is a deep, shadowed gully formed by the erosion of narrow zones of weaker rock. This is one of the classic rock-climbing cliffs in the Lake District, worthy of comparison with Scafell Crag and Pillar Rock.

From the outlet of Goats Water, cross the steep scree slope and keep on past a boulder cave, which can provide useful shelter, to the foot of the crag at the base of C Buttress. There is a choice of routes here: the easier way contours round to the right past Intermediate Gully, where a small spring is usually flowing, and across scree to the ridge near Goats Hause. This route misses out the top of Dow Crag, and a better alternative is to turn left at the base of C Buttress and seek out Wainwright's scrambling way up South Rake to the summit ridge. Keeping to the base of the main crags, the route passes the narrow cleft of Great Gully and the entrance to Easy Gully before climbing steeply on scree in exciting surroundings to reach the main ridge.

From the top of South Rake the rocky summit of **Dow Crag** (2,555ft) is easily gained along the ridge, with magnificent views northwards along the plunging line of crags and eastwards across Goats Water to the Old Man of Coniston. The little tor forming the summit is an excellent vantage point for the main ridge of the Coniston Fells, with the Scafell range away to the left; from the path down to the col of Goat's Hause the conical top of Harter Fell in Eskdale is particularly prominent across the deep hollow containing Seathwaite Tarn, Barrow's reservoir.

After some initial steepness over rough ground, the way from Goat's Hause to the top of the **Old Man of Coniston** (2,633ft) becomes an easy stroll on grass, curving gently south-east across a broad upland sheep pasture. The summit is dramatically sited above the corrie tarn of Low Water, and the badly worn track coming up from the tarn is clearly visible. The highest of the Coniston Fells, the Old Man has to suffer the consequences, and the summit, noted for its fine views south and east over the estuaries of the Kent, Leven and Duddon and along the full length of Coniston Water, is often crowded. The summit cairn, built on a considerable platform which also serves as a wind-shelter, suffers regularly at the hands of vandals; the adjacent OS column is more resilient.

Most of the hard work on this first day's walk is now over, and a fair speed can be achieved on the straightforward ridge walk to the rounded dome of **Brim Fell** (2,611ft), notable on my last visit only for the impressively large pile of stones marking its summit since the top was shrouded in a thin layer of mist which agonisingly failed to clear, although blue sky and a very hazy sun were visible directly above. The featureless descent to Levers Hause, the only significant break in the main ridge of the Coniston Fells, can be completed equally quickly, but the pull up past the rocky turrets of Little How Crags (where there

Coniston Fells from
Pike O'Blisco

are disused mineral workings) and Great How Crags demands a
more circumspect approach. Down on the right, at the base of
Great How Crags and overlooking Levers Water (converted into
a reservoir for the long-disused copper mines) is a good example
of a goose-bield, a cunning if somewhat cruel device for trapping
foxes. The rough stone walls which imprisoned over-inquisitive
foxes still stand to a height of several feet.

The extensive summit plateau of **Swirl How** (2,630ft) is easily
gained above the top of Great How Crags. There is a fine view
from the cairn, at the edge of the Greenburn valley and at the top
of the ridge of Prison Band. An unjustly neglected fell, Swirl
How is only 3ft lower than the Old Man of Coniston and is the
true centre of the Coniston Fells; there are fine routes, too, to its
summit from Greenburn.

The final two summits on this walk can now be picked off
very easily. **Great Carrs** (2,575ft) is less than half a mile away
across grassy slopes. The route contours around the head of the
Greenburn Beck valley, with the shattered rim of Broad Slack – a
vast combe containing the sparse wreckage of an aeroplane which
narrowly failed to clear the ridge – on the right. By this stage the
northerly prospect, embracing the Scafell group, Crinkle Crags

and Bowfell, is superb, but it is worth waiting until **Grey Friar** (2,536ft) has been climbed before savouring the view at leisure. The route from Great Carrs dips down to the col at Fairfield and gradually climbs the gentle upper slopes of Grey Friar, a comparatively uninteresting peak in itself but widely known for its magnificent view north-west of the entire Scafell range, from Slight Side to Great End, across the desolate waste of upper Eskdale. Westwards is the shapely peak of Harter Fell, and to the south-east is a fine panorama of the fells traversed during the day, with the Old Man of Coniston and Dow Crag separated by the prominent trough of Goat's Hause.

Two rock outcrops enliven the summit scene on Grey Friar, with a little mild scrambling possible on the lower, northerly one, and the way down to Cockley Beck initially twists and turns between a series of outcrops before reaching easier ground above the headwaters of the (tautologically named) Cockley Beck Gill. The key to the descent is the junction of walls at about 1,700ft, nearly half a mile north-west of the summit. Once this has been found an intermittent path can be picked up, leading down the north-east bank of the beck (or gill!) past disused copper workings to the isolated farmhouse (probably once an inn catering for the busy packhorse trade) at **Cockley Beck**.

The junction of minor roads at Cockley Beck is an important one. To the east are Wrynose Pass and Little Langdale; southwards lies the road to Seathwaite and the Duddon valley. West, across Cockley Beck Bridge, a delightful single-arched bridge spanning the River Duddon, is the road across Hardknott Pass to Eskdale. Leave this road immediately west of the bridge and follow the obvious track close to the river bank as far as Black Hall. This track is on the line of the Roman road between Galava (Ambleside) and Glannaventa (Ravenglass), and indeed for the next two miles the Horseshoe route is the same as that taken by the Roman Way and a full description is given under that route.

The former farmhouse of Black Hall is now a youth hostel, and is conveniently placed to serve as an overnight halt for YHA members. Other accommodation is almost non-existent in this lonely area, however, and the best strategy is to follow the zigzag path from Black Hall to the top of Hardknott Pass. At 1,291ft above sea level, the pass is guarded by a number of difficult hairpin bends and the approach roads reach a maximum gradient of 1 in 3; casualties and the resultant traffic jams are a common irritant for summer drivers.

Just to the west of Hardknott Pass a path strikes north-west across the bracken below the small crags of Border End, aiming for the parade ground of the **Hardknott Roman Fort**. From here the fort itself is reached by a simple descent of the gentle slope above the crags of Bell Stand. The fort is well worth an extended exploration, since the foundations of the main buildings have been carefully restored by the Department of the Environment (see the Roman Way for details). Just south-west of the fort the path can be picked up again as it heads back to the road, which can be followed steeply down to the farmhouse at Brotherilkeld; alternatively, a right of way leaves the path shortly before it regains the road, and descends equally steeply close to Bell Stand to reach the riverside path near the farmhouse. Limited accommodation is available at the farms in upper Eskdale, but the nearest inn, The Woolpack (its name betrays its origins) is a weary mile or so further down the valley.

2 UPPER ESKDALE AND THE SCAFELL RANGE
Brotherilkeld to Wasdale Head (10 miles/16km)

The farmhouse of **Brotherilkeld**, which forms the starting point for the second leg of the Lakeland Horseshoe, has the long, low outline typical of the great seventeenth-century age of rebuilding in the Lake District, but its history goes back much further than that. Indeed, it seems probable that this is the earliest of all the great dalehead sheep farms. Brotherilkeld means 'the booth of Ulfkell', booth being Norse for a hut or summer shelter, and it is likely that right from the Scandinavian settlement of the valley to the present day it has been the highest farm in Eskdale.

In 1242 Furness Abbey bought the farm, comprising an incredible 14,000 acres of rough grazing stretching from the Roman road to Esk Hause, five miles away at the head of the valley. Some forty years later John de Hudleston, lord of the manor of Millom, allowed the monks to enclose the sheep pastures, and remains of this early medieval boundary can be seen later on the route. By the seventeenth century ownership had passed to a 'statesman', one of a new breed of rural middle-class yeoman farmers, and as his prosperity grew he was able to rebuild the farmhouse in the distinctive style which first emerged in late Tudor times and which has become a classic feature of the landscape of the Lake District. Nowadays the farm, together with nearby Taw House and Penny Hill farms, is in the ownership of the National Trust; it is also the location for the Eskdale show, usually held on the last Saturday in September.

The Lakeland Horseshoe takes the footpath close to the east bank of the Esk and at first follows the course of the river upstream through lowland pastures. It is interesting to reflect that if the Forestry Commission, who bought the land in 1935, had had their way walkers using this path would be picking their way through the Hardknott Forest Park. It was only after eight years of concerted and widespread opposition to their plans that the Commission entered into a covenant with the National Trust in which they agreed not to plant around Brotherilkeld. As a result the landscape today is virtually treeless away from the river, and only the name of Yew Crags, the prominent rocky bluff above the scree slopes on the right, remains as evidence that yews were once abundant in this area; centuries of grazing have stripped the fellside of trees.

The path rises gently through a series of terraces – former lake beds now being eroded by the river – and past an obvious old river channel, about a quarter of a mile above Brotherilkeld, before beginning to climb more steadily through wilder country, although still keeping close to the river. The view left of the unusual profile of Heron Crag on the west bank of the Esk is matched to the right by a view of the Steeple, a detached pillar of rock some fifty feet high on the flank of Hard Knott. The Steeple

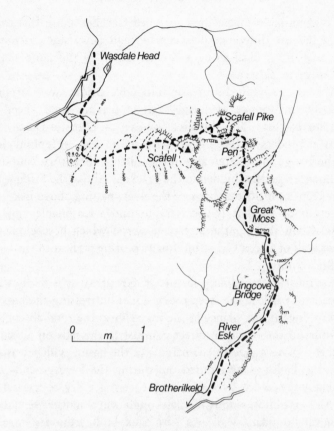

is sometimes awarded the somewhat fanciful title of the Eskdale
Needle, though the resemblance between this rather squat tower
and the more famous Napes Needle, in its magnificent surroundings on Great Gable, is slight.

Just above the confluence of the Esk with Lingcove Beck, the
route forks left by a sheepfold (the path to the right leads to
Three Tarns and Bowfell or to an interesting scramble up
Yeastyrigg Gill to Ore Gap and Esk Pike) and crosses Lingcove
Beck on a simple, narrow but attractive single-arched packhorse
bridge. The description 'ageless' takes on a new significance
when it is realised that **Lingcove Bridge**, seemingly ancient, is
a comparatively recent piece of work. The old bridge was
gradually weakened by successive floods and eventually collapsed;

yet it is unlikely that even a seasoned traveller along this route could tell the difference between old and new, since each was fashioned from local stone and constructed to the same simple but effective pattern.

A predecessor of the present Lingcove Bridge was certainly used by the monks of Furness when driving their sheep to summer pastures, and this area, known as Throstle Garth, has many reminders of those days, with the monks' sheepfold close by the bridge and the remains of the thirteenth-century boundary of the sheep pasture hidden in the bracken. Above the bridge, the path keeps near the east bank of the river, passing above Esk Falls (a detour to the left is necessary to find a reasonable view of these), then skirting the attractive gorge which lies below the gaunt wall of Green Crag, and finally bearing right into the basin of Great Moss.

The most extraordinary feature of **Great Moss** is its location immediately below the steep rocky slopes buttressing the highest land in England. A glance at the map shows the total absence of contours in the Moss, in direct contrast to the fells on all sides. And this gives a clue to the origins of the basin, which was the site of a shallow lake scoured out during the Ice Age and then gradually succeeded by a peat bog. Steering a dry course across the Moss is almost impossible, although when another stretch of medieval boundary wall – a turf bank built around a core of rough boulders – is encountered, it is prudent to follow its course, approximately parallel to the river. The form of the medieval boundary is interesting: the agreement in 1284 allowed Furness Abbey to erect a structure which would restrict the movement of sheep but permit deer to roam freely, and so the monks chose to build the low wall and dyke which is still faintly in evidence today.

Having negotiated Great Moss, the Horseshoe walker has to cross the wide and usually shallow River Esk. This can be difficult after rain, but in dry weather the river can easily be forded near the confluence with How Beck. The terrain changes abruptly as height is gained, from boggy peat to bouldery scree. Indeed, some of the boulders just downstream are so large that they have attracted the attention of cartographers and are marked on the map as Sampson's Stones. The rock scenery in this part of upper Eskdale is magnificent: above and to the left is the forbidding shattered wall of Cam Spout Crag, with the waterfalls of Cam Spout to the right, and further up the main valley is the startling bulk of Esk Buttress (called Dow Crag on Ordnance Survey maps).

There is a choice of three routes to the top of Scafell Pike from this point. Perhaps the least rewarding follows the river below Esk Buttress and then climbs the steep and unpleasantly stony gully of Little Narrowcove to the col between Broad Crag and Scafell Pike. Although there are intimate views of the towering southern cliffs of Ill Crag, the route is for the most part confined within the depths of Little Narrowcove, and the ascent of the shifting scree can be pure torture. Another way is the orthodox route which heads for the gorge and waterfalls of Cam Spout, with a steep scramble up past the falls and a tiring climb over troublesome loose scree to the deep gash of Mickledore, from where Scafell Pike is easily gained.

More interesting, and a good deal less stony initially, is the untracked route which rises diagonally from the Esk above the left shoulder of Esk Buttress and across a sloping grassy shelf to reach the virtually unknown peak of **Pen**. Only its remote situation on this 'hidden' side of Scafell Pike denies Pen, with its really delightful rocky summit overlooking upper Eskdale, the recognition it deserves, although with a height of over 2,500ft and a wild, rocky grandeur to match, it perhaps ought to be visited by all true Lakeland connoisseurs. Not far above Pen, but reached only by a strenuous, steep scramble, as is usual in this vicinity, is another outlying summit of Scafell Pike. This is Rough Crag, below which an easy traverse leads to the upper section of the scree shoot in Little Narrowcove. From the col a left turn and a rather trying walk over the inevitable boulder field leads to the summit of Scafell Pike.

One final route, which should appeal to the adventurous but should only be attempted by experienced fell walkers, is the steep, rocky scramble from Rough Crag directly up the Eskdale face of Scafell Pike. Previous guidebook writers have been unduly cautious about this route but, although there are no paths, there should be few problems if the more exposed and craggy areas below the summit are avoided. One possibility is to set a course for Broadcrag Tarn – the highest tarn in the Lake District, yet hardly visited on its shelf away from the main tourist routes across the summit plateau – and then to climb north-east to the summit past the remains of a Stone Age axe factory (covering about four acres and littered with rough axe-heads but rather less impressive than the more famous example on Pike o' Stickle). It should be emphasised, however, that the stony wastes above Rough Crag are pathless and that, although the ascent of England's highest mountain by this rather unconventional route can be uniquely rewarding, it should definitely be avoided in all but clear weather and by walkers unaccustomed to compass work and rock scrambling.

The top of **Scafell Pike** (3,206ft), with its huge and usually thickly populated summit cairn, is a disappointment for many on their first visit. The bleak summit plateau is a barren mass of boulders, and the cairn itself, partly collapsed, has lost much of its original attraction, although the steps leading up to the platform on top are still there. There is a strange atmosphere of neglect about the place, stemming partly from the ruined shelters and partly from the accumulated rubbish of so many visitors. And too often, of course, the saving grace of the summit, the all-embracing view, is lost in mist or rain. Nevertheless, this is still the highest land in England, and if the top itself is unimpressive, the mountain as a whole has a rugged and often dramatic quality which few others can equal.

The next objective on this second stage of the Horseshoe walk, Scafell, is close at hand but surprisingly difficult to set foot upon. The route is straightforward at first, down the obvious path across the boulders to the col of Mickledore, formed of rocks less resistant to erosion than those on either side, but at the far end the cliff of Broad Stand (an easy rock climb but out of the question for walkers) enforces a diversion either to left or right, with an inevitable loss of height and hence a more energy-sapping ascent of Scafell.

Pikes Crag and Scafell Crag

Before considering the best means of further progress, it is well worth while to pause to take in the magnificent rock scenery. Behind, Pikes Crag, solidly buttressing the summit wastes of Scafell Pike, is instantly recognisable by the gullies deeply etched across its face and by the prominent Pulpit Rock. To the right are steep scree slopes leading down to the upland basin of Hollow Stones and the easy route (useful if bad weather prevents the climb to the top of Scafell) via Brown Tongue to Wasdale Head. In front is the formidable face of Scafell Crag, the most stupendous display of naked rock in the country— a series of steeply angled buttresses separated by wild black gullies which, facing north, rarely see the sun.

Returning to the ascent of Scafell, the diversion to the left uses the Eskdale path, dropping steeply down towards Cam Spout for a short distance before taking the gully slanting upwards and skirting the fringe of East Buttress. At the top of the gully is Foxes Tarn, the second highest in the Lake District but rather a nondescript pool and probably the smallest to bear a name. The summit is only a short distance above the tarn. The other, more exciting, possibility facing the walker at Mickledore is to turn right and head for the foot of the dramatic angled scree shoot of Lord's Rake, either across the scree well below Scafell Crag or by means of the climbers' traverse known as Rake's Progress, an exhilarating route entailing some scrambling and needing a steady head, since there is a tricky and rather exposed section shortly after leaving Mickledore.

Safely arrived at the foot of Lord's Rake, the walker now embarks upon one of the best rock scrambles in the Lake District. The Rake rises diagonally for about two hundred yards across the right-hand side of Scafell Crag, starting at the foot of Deep Gill and emerging on the broad top of Scafell some way north-west of the summit cairn. The first section of the Rake is a broad scree gully climbing between the main bulk of Scafell Crag and the lower Shamrock Buttress, which forms a reassuring outer wall. The scree in the trench is extremely loose and progress may well be painfully slow; indeed, the Lake District Special Planning Board warned years ago that the route had become so badly eroded that it was dangerous in places. The problem is the sheer volume of people seeking out what is unquestionably the finest way to the top of Scafell, and short of closing the Rake or constructing an artificial rock staircase, actions which would be anathema to most fell walkers, there is little that can be done to improve the condition of the Rake.

The scree gully ends at a miniature col (the West Wall Traverse, a variation finish, leads off to the left just before this point and makes for the stony upper section of Deep Gill) and Lord's Rake keeps straight ahead, descending slightly and then rising gently to the summit plateau. From the exit of the Rake the broad track can be followed left to the summit of **Scafell** (3,162ft), marked by a solid cairn and the much less solid ruin of a wind-shelter. The summit is set well back from the craggy north face of the fell and suffers badly from this since there is little of interest nearby, but the exceptional view south is a great consolation. Morecambe Bay, the Duddon estuary, the Coniston Fells and the length of Eskdale from Esk Pike to the estuary at Ravenglass are all displayed impressively in a broad arc. The mountain scenery, obstructed by the massive dome of Scafell Pike, is less spectacular, but becomes more interesting during the descent to Wasdale Head.

From the summit cairn the route heads back towards the top of Lord's Rake, but then curves left along a good path above Black Crag to the grassy shoulder of Green How. Wastwater, Wordsworth's 'long, narrow, stern and desolate lake', now fills the view to the left, and ahead are the craggy summits dominating Mosedale. The path becomes intermittent here but the general direction down towards Groove Gill is clear; eventually it joins the Old Corpse Road along which the dead were at one time carried from Wasdale Head across Burnmoor for burial at the chapel at Boot in Eskdale. This track is followed to the right, across Lingmell Gill and Lingmell Beck to the main valley road leading to the hamlet of **Wasdale Head**. The ascent of the Scafells having almost certainly been a tiring expedition, the Horseshoe walker may well delay an exploration of the features of interest around here (and there are several, details of which are included in the Valley Route itinerary) in order to enjoy a well-earned glass of real ale in The Wasdale Head Inn.

3 PILLAR AND THE HIGH STILE RANGE
Wasdale Head to Buttermere (13 miles/21km)

The first half of the Mosedale Horseshoe, justifiably regarded as the most rewarding walk of its kind in the Lake District, is the first objective of this strenuous day, which involves tough climbs to two ridges: the steep ascent from Wasdale Head to Red Pike (Wasdale) and then, after a descent into the remote dalehead of Ennerdale, another stiff climb onto the spine of the High Stile range. The route leaves Wasdale Head by crossing the simple but practical packhorse bridge behind The Wasdale Head Inn. Row Head Bridge may seem nowadays to serve little purpose, but previously the road up the valley from Strands followed the north bank of Mosedale Beck until entering the hamlet over this bridge. Beyond the bridge a wide path enclosed by drystone

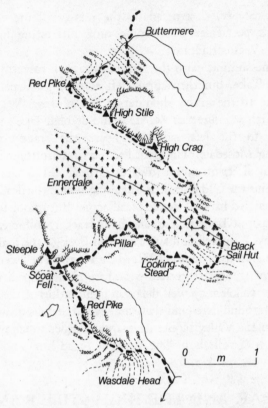

walls heads up Mosedale, with tremendous views to the right of Great Gable and Great End, and the beck cascading below over Ritson Force, named after a former landlord of the inn.

Beyond the fell gate the green path keeps to the valley bottom, and although the shortest route reaching the ridge at the col of Dore Head strikes diagonally and very stonily up the northern slopes of Yewbarrow here, it is preferable to remain on the lower path until the col, a striking dip in the skyline between the notched rocks of Stirrup Crag on the slopes of Yewbarrow and Bull Crags below Red Pike (Wasdale), is directly above. A desperate and seemingly unending climb is then unavoidable, through bracken and then on grass and loose, sliding rock, keeping to the right to avoid the worst of the scree.

Loose rock is more or less inevitable in the higher part of the climb, but life becomes pleasanter once Dore Head is reached. A ridge walk in excellent scenery, with the occasional opportunity for a bit of rock scrambling, is now in prospect. On the left Scoat Tarn comes into view, set in a surprisingly green and pleasant hollow but with a rocky shoreline emphasising its situation close to the great fells of the Pillar range. On the other side of the ridge is the wild head of Mosedale below the sombre crags of Red Pike. And the retrospective view over Wasdale Head and Wastwater to the extraordinary rock walls guarding Scafell and Scafell Pike is superb – best seen, incidentally, from the venerable feature known as the Chair, a cairn south of the summit ingeniously constructed against a rock outcrop.

The grassy summit of **Red Pike** (2,707ft) is now only a gentle stroll away. The cairn is attractively positioned right on the edge of the precipitous drop into Mosedale. The route continues above the edge of the cliffs towards **Scoat Fell** (2,760ft), a fine peak but rather tame in comparison with its even finer neighbours. The last few hundred yards are dull but easy, over a stony and gently sloping fell top. The summit cairn is perched rather oddly astride a well-built but now crumbling wall, and a few yards north another cairn, rather better sited, points the way towards Steeple. The wall which crosses Scoat Fell is part of the boundary fence which once followed the whole of the Ennerdale watershed, and further traces of it – either as a wall or a fence – are seen later in the day.

The next section of the route, a half-mile round trip, can be omitted if the weather is deteriorating but in all other circumstances it should certainly be included. This short digression is a challenging scramble along the narrow ridge northwards from Scoat Fell to the small but exquisite summit of **Steeple** (2,687ft), with superb views down into Mirk Cove and Mirklin Cove, the deep and ravaged corries on either side of the arête. Strictly speaking, Steeple is part of Scoat Fell but the aptly named peak at the end of the ridge has far more character than its parent fell. The summit cairn is perched on the very edge of the crags, with marvellous views down into the coves and, to the west, along the length of Ennerdale.

Returning to the top of Scoat Fell, the Lakeland Horseshoe heads east above Black Crag, with its unsurpassed view back to the precipitous cliffs falling away below the summit of Steeple, and then down to Wind Gap, an excellent high-level col. At 2,480ft this is the highest point on the direct route from Wasdale to Ennerdale, a way much used in parts nowadays but rarely followed along its whole length. Keep to the ridge path as it climbs the steep, bouldery slope onto the grassy tableland of **Pillar** (2,927ft), which has a summit which is remarkably gentle compared with the savage rock scenery characteristic of its Ennerdale face. The ruinous wire fence untidily crossing the summit area, which numbers amongst its artefacts an Ordnance Survey column, two wind-shelters and numerous cairns, hardly adds to the charm of the area. Visiting the summit is only the prelude, however, to the much more exciting descent of the mountain by the High-Level Route, with close-up views of the awesome precipice of Pillar Rock.

The way lies north to the second wind-shelter (from where there is a superb view of the top of Pillar Rock, detached from the fellside and standing proudly above the appalling Ennerdale plantations) and then, heading towards Pisgah, the first of the Rock's buttresses, carefully down a fairly steep scree slope to the prominent stretcher box. A right turn here signals the start of the Shamrock Traverse, a comfortable if rather exposed walk above magnificent crags. From the far end of the traverse the route is well marked and straightforward to Robinson's Cairn. The cairn, a memorial to John Wilson Robinson, a pioneer rock climber who first scaled Pillar Rock in 1882 and made more than a hundred ascents of the mountain, was first built on Easter Saturday 1908, but sadly has become a regular target for cairn-wreckers.

Perhaps the most notable feature of Robinson's Cairn is its location as the ideal viewpoint for the east face of Pillar Rock, and, with all the difficulties of the High-Level Route already out of the way, a leisurely contemplation of the precipice has certainly been earned. First climbed in 1826 by a local shepherd called John Atkinson, the Rock has grown in reputation ever since, both with rock climbers – who have put up some notably fine and fearsomely difficult routes – and walkers, who can see the entire 500ft drop from High Man to the green ledge north of Savage Gully. The twin tops of Pisgah and High Man, the lesser peak of Low Man and the remarkable buttresses separated by brooding deep clefts represent a perfection of rock architecture which almost defies description.

From Robinson's Cairn follow the obvious path crossing Hind Cove and Green Cove to reach the main path (and more rusty boundary posts) shortly before the summit of **Looking Stead** (2,058ft), a good vantage point for the drab Forestry Commission plantations in Ennerdale. In the early twentieth century Ennerdale was described by A. G. Bradley in *Highways and Byways in the Lake District* as 'a wild trough-like valley untouched by civilisation, and threaded by the windings of a silver stream'. Now, the stream is barely visible and the wildness is lost forever beneath the trees since 'civilisation', in the form of the Forestry Commission, arrived in 1925 and began to plant Norway spruce below Windgap Cove in the following year. The Commission now owns nearly 9,000 acres here, although nearly half, including Pillar Rock and Great Gable, is leased to the National Trust, an agreement having been wrung out of them in 1935 to the effect that the central fells would never be planted.

However, the 4,000 acres of spruce and larch, planted in geometric blocks with no regard to the effect on the landscape, still affronts the dignity of the superb fellsides around Pillar, and worse may follow with clear felling beginning in earnest, denuding sections of the plantations until the fruits of replanting become visible. The result is that Ennerdale is probably the quietest of the Lake District's major valleys, neglected because of its dismal shroud of conifers and despite the belated efforts to encourage recreation in the lower valley. The dale has, indeed, always been quiet: a medieval hunting preserve, it could have been opened up during the railway age, but proposals for a line up the valley were defeated in 1884, and Ennerdale Water (a mere remnant of the vast Ice Age lake which filled an over-deepened basin scoured out by glaciers) and the valley of the

River Liza remain largely unvisited.

The Lakeland Horseshoe, close to the dalehead, reaches the River Liza by way of the track coming down from Black Sail Pass (where there are the forlorn remains of a gateway) by the side of Sail Beck. It then passes the **Black Sail Hut**, formerly a three-roomed shepherds' bothy but now converted to squeeze in eighteen youth hostellers thirsting for the simple life. Six miles from the end of the valley road and with few concessions to the twentieth century, it is in a marvellous position with Pillar, Kirkfell, Great Gable, Haystacks and High Crag crying out to be climbed. Beyond the hostel the pace is likely to slacken even though the second main climb of the day, at least as far as Scarth Gap, is a fairly easy stroll by the edge of the plantations. At the pass there was another gate, this time part of the boundary of Gatesgarth Farm, which can soon be seen down in the valley, at the head of Buttermere. The adjacent car park will probably be full, and the footpath from Gatesgarth to Scarth Gap is likely to be busy, showing the effects of its popularity in litter and general wear and tear.

At Scarth Gap the character of the walk changes from a gentle stroll to a hard slog. The way lies left, up an unpleasant scree slope, to the craggy little summit of Seat, and then across grass down to a hollow containing a couple of rather odd tarns. The next ascent is the ridge of Gamlin End, which starts easily past the Marble Stone, identifiable from its embedded boundary post, but soon deteriorates and ends with a desperate scramble up very unstable and completely unavoidable scree. Just occasionally tufts of heather or grass and outcrops of reasonably firm rock give some respite from the fine, loose scree, but generally the climb is arduous and depressingly slow. Frequent stops are likely, and fortunately the scenery is good enough to make them worth while, although Pillar Rock is difficult to pick out, especially against the sun. The head of Ennerdale presents a wild, lonely appearance, with Haystacks looking surprisingly dull (certainly from this angle the accolades which it has received in the past seem over-generous) in contrast with Great Gable, which as always is prominent and compelling.

When, finally, the east ridge of High Crag is gained, the Buttermere valley and the smoothly sculptured Newlands fells come into view. The path swings left up to the rocky summit of **High Crag** (2,443ft), with the Grasmoor fells now well in view beyond Crummock Water. From the southern edge of the bouldery plateau Ennerdale Water and the lonely fells of Kinniside can be seen, and to the south-east is probably the best view of the head of Ennerdale, with the Scafell range behind. The High Street and Helvellyn ridges fill the eastern horizon beyond Fleetwith Pike.

The Horseshoe route now takes a spectacular traverse around the lip of the vast hollow of Birkness Comb, a corrie basin without a tarn but ringed by dramatic crags and situated above the hanging valley of Comb Beck. The route is easily followed (the fence posts are an infallible but superfluous guide) to **High Stile** (2,644ft), the highest point on the ridge. The summit comes as an anticlimax, however, after the ridge walk with its intimate views of the shattered cliff of Eagle Crag and its array of gullies and buttresses.

The view more than compensates for any disappointment at the lack of interesting features on the rough, flat top; it is especially notable to the north-east, with Grasmoor and the ridge from Eel Crag to Causey Pike overtopped by Skiddaw and Blencathra. There is also a fine view from the western edge of the plateau directly down into Bleaberry Comb, the hollow between High Stile and Red Pike (Buttermere). Bleaberry Tarn (created by ice erosion and a resultant over-deepened hollow, and not, as Robert Southey once suggested, the crater of an extinct volcano) and Crummock Water provide most interest here. This view is somewhat marred, though, by the red gash across the breast of Red Pike where heavy use of the 'tourist route' from Buttermere has torn away the vegetation to expose and gradually erode the underlying rocks.

These red screes are conspicuous during the walk, mostly on turf, along the ridge above Chapel Crags and slanting right across rocks to reach the finely situated cairn on the graceful summit of **Red Pike** (2,479ft). The rock here, too, has a reddish

Red Pike (Buttermere)
from High Stile

tinge for most of the mountain is composed of an igneous intrusion. The main effect on the scenery is to produce mostly rounded slopes on Red Pike and its lower neighbour, Dodd, which contrast vividly with the craggy, broken terrain on the Borrowdale Volcanics of High Stile. From Red Pike to Buttermere village there is a choice of four routes, none of them without disadvantages. The popular way down to Bleaberry Tarn is in a terrible state, but is the most direct; the Ling Comb route is hard work across pathless heather for some distance; Lingcomb Edge presents some difficulties in path-finding; and the Scale Force route is a tedious line of descent and at this stage in the day's walk is too circuitous to merit serious consideration. Discarding Ling Comb and Scale Force, the other possibilities are described in turn.

My own preference is for Lingcomb Edge, which has excellent views of Mellbreak and Crummock Water ahead during the descent and the added advantage of relative peace and quiet. The edge leaves the summit plateau to the north-west, and an intermittent path, with occasional cairns, picks its way down above a line of crags to the right. This straightforward descent comes to an abrupt halt above small crags at about 1,200ft, but a path can be picked up to the right heading for the obvious gap in the wall running up the fellside. From the wall a beeline can be made for the shore of Crummock Water, just south-east of Scale Island, although some diversions will be necessary to avoid the worst of the bracken. The lakeside path can then be taken to Scale Bridge and the village of Buttermere.

The other descent from Red Pike leaves the summit cairn in the direction of Bleaberry Tarn, then bears left down a very steep rocky section before the slope eases on the way down to the Saddle, between Red Pike and Dodd. The whole of this part of the route is very badly eroded, and with the prospect of more to come there is a case even at this stage for heading down into Ling Comb. Nevertheless, there is a fine view of Bleaberry Tarn and the gaunt, intimidating Chapel Crags, and the route does improve for a while as it crosses Sourmilk Gill and bears right down a gentle gradient to a cairn with a fine prospect of Fleetwith Pike at the head of Buttermere. A second very slippery scree slope follows, and even when Burtness Wood is reached the torture continues as the path angles down on slippery boulders. There are occasional tantalising glimpses through the trees of the lake, still far below at first, and a good deal of hard work is needed before the lakeside path is reached. Turn left here and cross Sourmilk Gill on a substantial wooden footbridge. (The piles of stones in the stream bed are testimony to the ferocity of the gill after winter storms, and indeed the sides and bed of the gill were gouged out afresh only a few years ago by a savage landslide.) A lane now leads across the alluvial flat to the village of **Buttermere**.

The village, with a few farms, a cluster of cottages and two hotels, is picturesque but of no particular interest. The tiny nineteenth-century church, sited above the village where the road over to Newlands leaves the valley, has a superb view of the lake. Originally Buttermere and Crummock Water formed a single lake, but the deposition of sediment on the intervening rock bar caused an eventual separation; later this alluvial flat became the common field of the village. Buttermere has all but succumbed to tourism, and the two inns, The Bridge, formerly called The Victoria and before that a corn mill, and The Fish, do a roaring summer trade. The four-mile circuit of Buttermere lake is an interesting diversion, but after the long and strenuous journey from Wasdale Head a quiet evening might be a more realistic proposition.

4   THE NORTH-WESTERN FELLS AND KESWICK
Buttermere to Keswick (12 miles/19km)

The Lakeland Horseshoe takes the Cockermouth road climbing steeply out of Buttermere, then bears right on a good path immediately after the last house on the right, at Crag Houses. Leave this path, which leads to Sail Pass, after about two-hundred-and-fifty yards and strike up the fellside through bracken and, higher up, some slaty outcrops. A prominent cairn marks the head of Rannerdale, an attractive and secluded valley down on the left. Lower down Rannerdale there was a medieval settlement, with its own chapel dedicated to the Blessed Mary Magdalene. Neither chapel nor hamlet has survived; the place was deserted in the seventeenth or eighteenth century. Now only the faint mounds of former farmsteads are left below the slate-grey screes of Grasmoor.

From the Rannerdale col the path ascends the shoulder of Whiteless Pike, passing a ruined sheepfold before gaining the main ridge, where a tremendous prospect opens up of the upper valley of Sail Beck, dominated by Causey Pike, the final peak to be tackled today. The retrospective view of the central fells above the placid lake of Buttermere is equally absorbing. Gradually the slope becomes more pronounced and the path zigzags on grass to the summit of **Whiteless Pike** (2,159ft), small and nicely situated above the steep upper fellside and noted for its excellent outlook southwards to the Scafell range. The route now lies north-east down to the col of Saddle Gate and up an excellent narrow ridge, dropping steeply down towards Third Gill on the

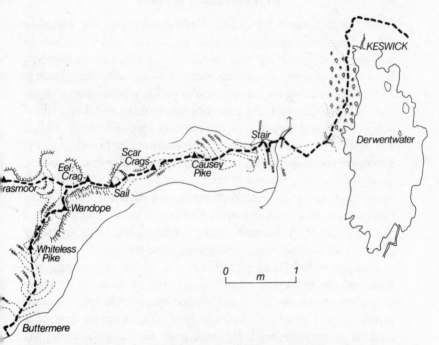

right and Rannerdale Beck on the left to the cairn on Thirdgill Head Man, and then across an upland sheep pasture to **Wandope** (2,533ft), perched above the massive corrie basin of Addacomb Hole. Wandope is a rather formless mountain, simply a point on the edge of a gently inclined grassy plateau, but has a fine prospect south-eastwards across a succession of ridges as far as Helvellyn.

North-west from Wandope, the route recrosses the large and featureless plateau to a cairn above the headwaters of Rannerdale Beck and then reaches a junction of paths in a grassy hollow containing some small pools and follows a well-cairned track for a dull but very easy half mile across gentle slopes to the flat top of **Grasmoor** (2,791ft), the highest of the north-western fells. This line of approach hardly does justice to Grasmoor, which from Crummock Water appears as a dramatic, craggy peak, but the detour is worth while for the wide panorama available from the summit, especially to the south and west, where the fells form a superb backcloth to the blue waters of Buttermere, Crummock

Water and Loweswater. The Helvellyn range, the Langdale Pikes, the Coniston Fells, Bowfell and Great Gable, the Scafells and the summit of Pillar seen above the High Stile range combine to present a picture of startling complexity and absorbing beauty.

Before returning to the junction of paths, venture north to the rim of Dove Crags, a fine precipice overlooking the deep cleft of Gasgale Gill and, beyond, Whiteside and Hopegill Head. This is the only real excitement near the summit, although for the geologist there are stone stripes and stone polygons, resulting from frost action, littered about the summit plateau. Others will hurry back across the excellent turf in the direction of Eel Crag (called Crag Hill on OS maps), slanting over to the right for a second look at Addacomb Hole, a marvellous hanging valley with a backdrop of crags eating back into the summit plateau.

The top of **Eel Crag** (2,749ft) is a stony but surprisingly flat area, and the main interest is concentrated to the east, with the crag after which the fell is named and the narrow ridge leading down to Sail much in evidence here. The ridge is one of a number of ways to reach Keswick from Eel Crag (another, via Grisedale Pike, forms part of the North-Western Fells route), and many will consider it the best. It starts with the superb narrow ridge leading to **Sail** (2,530ft), an unassuming peak which has flanks characterised by long grassy slopes and a summit with no intrinsic interest which lies slightly away from the main path.

The path continues easily down a similarly narrow ridge to Sail Pass, a high level col on the route between Buttermere and Braithwaite with, on the left, the desolate workings of Force Crag mine (reopened in the 1970s to work barytes) scarring the head of Coledale below the impressive double buttress of Force Crag itself. Even closer, below Long Crag, is a long-abandoned cobalt mine. The mine road, which gives a well-graded alternative route to Stair, can be seen leading below Long Crag towards the valley of Stonycroft Gill.

The connoisseurs' route, however, continues along the ridge, first visiting the top of **Scar Crags** (2,205ft), which has an interesting rocky summit ridge perched above cliffs and sliding scree falling towards the deep valley of Rigg Beck. The obvious track along the crest passes above a succession of thrusting buttresses and sombre gullies before dropping down to an insignificant depression and rising to the equally attractive serrated summit ridge of **Causey Pike** (2,035ft). There are five distinct little peaks on this rough but delightful fell top, and the highest requires a scramble over rocks before it can be conquered.

The view from Causey Pike is excellent, with the valleys of Newlands Beck and the River Derwent complemented by the grouping of Dale Head, Hindscarth and Robinson opposite the Catbells ridge; Skiddaw and Blencathra displayed above Keswick and Derwentwater; and the ridge to Eel Crag which has just been descended forming an imposing obstacle to the west. But what sets this attractive and accessible mountain apart are the views *to* Causey Pike; from almost any direction the turreted crest is instantly recognisable, throwing down an irresistible invitation. And this inevitably causes its own problems. Loneliness is not one of Causey Pike's characteristics, and there will generally be someone on the summit and plenty of people on the way up and down. Yet the mountain seems to cope better than most with the trampling feet, and the paths are not as badly eroded as its undoubted popularity would lead one to expect.

Leaving the highest of Causey Pike's turrets, the route heads east down a challenging slate outcrop to the col at Sleet Hause, with the views across Derwentwater becoming increasingly spectacular. The lake, three miles long and up to a mile and a half wide, is relatively shallow and has a central ridge which comes to the surface in St Herbert's Island (once the sanctuary of a hermit) and Derwent Isle. No place to be in a howling gale, with the rain clouds advancing menacingly over Robinson, the hause marks the divergence of two routes to Stair. One keeps to the ridge track through the heather as far as Rowling End and then drops sharply down to the valley of Stonycroft Gill; the other, perhaps slightly preferable, follows the wide path down to the left, slanting below the prominent spur of Rowling End and descending through bracken on a path which is sometimes stony and sometimes excellent turf.

Causey Pike and
the Stonycroft Gill valley

Pause towards the end of this descent to look back at the distinctive skyline from Causey Pike right to the dark eastern wall of Eel Crags at the head of Stonycroft Gill. Then, after the Rowling End route joins from the right, aim for the bridge crossing the gill, here in a deeply incised miniature gorge. Near the bridge was a lead mine first worked in the sixteenth century, though without much success. More profitable was the large lead smelter which was built by the gill, then called Smelt Mill Gill, in the seventeenth century to process ore from the Newlands mines. By the 1750s the smelter was in continuous production and lead ore was carried by packhorse from the Greenside mine, the most prolific in the Lake District, across Sticks Pass in the Helvellyn range for processing here. Just to the north of Stonycroft the spoil heaps of the Uzzicar lead and copper mine, dwarfed in the 1880s by a 60ft waterwheel, provide further evidence of the busy industrial history of this peaceful spot.

A few hundred yards further on, at the point where Stonycroft Gill joins Newlands Beck, is the hamlet of **Stair**, its farms and cottages attractively situated on both sides of the beck. The mill here was still rolling oats until the First World War, although it was last operated as a flour mill in the 1880s. One of the farm-houses has the date 1647 and the initials TF above a doorway, and it is reputed that Sir Thomas Fairfax, a leading Parliament-arian and one of Cromwell's generals, lived here for a while.

There is a direct road from Stair to Keswick, but this can (and in summer certainly should) be avoided by taking the signposted field path south-east to reach the farms at Skelgill, below the Catbells ridge. Low Skelgill is a fine example of a seventeenth-century statesman's farmhouse, though it is on the site of a much older building and there are signs of the ancient cruck trusses having been re-used as beams. Nearby is High Skelgill, a taller and more formal eighteenth-century dwelling. The route bears left at Skelgill, following the base of the fell to Hawse End and the extremely popular path from Catbells to Keswick via Silver Hill and the village of Portinscale. Near Silver Hill are the gardens at Lingholm, specialising in rhododendrons and azaleas and consequently at their best in early June.

Portinscale (the name is rather unexpectedly derived from the Old Norse for 'the prostitute's hut') is a fairly substantial village catering largely for tourists but relatively quiet since the A66 bypass was constructed. The Tower Hotel was originally built by a particularly prosperous mayor of Manchester in the 1860s. The River Derwent was formerly crossed by the picturesque Long Bridge at Portinscale; this was already built of stone by the early thirteenth century, but was progressively weakened by storm water and was partly washed away in the floods of 1955. A Bailey bridge filled the breach for some years, but now a suspension footbridge, functional but hardly appropriate for such a setting, carries pedestrians from the village towards the thriving centre of Keswick.

First, however, it is worth visiting Great Crosthwaite, on the opposite bank of the River Greta from the town itself, for this was the original settlement in the area, and its church was the centre of a parish which included most of Borrowdale. The church of St Kentigern is said to have been first built around 533 AD; certainly it was reconstructed in the twelfth, fourteenth and six-teenth centuries, and what stands today is undistinguished Late

Perpendicular in style apart from the north chapel. Even as late as 1306 it was to Crosthwaite that people came on Sundays to buy 'corn, flour, beans, peas, linen and cloth, fish and flesh'.

In contrast **Keswick**, which simply means 'dairy farm', was little more than that until about 1300, although twenty years earlier it had obtained a market charter from Edward I and this, allied to its location at the confluence of the Greta and the Derwent and astride the main valley routes through the Lake District, led to its steady growth into an important market centre. Industry, too, was important in promoting expansion, initially through mining enterprises in Borrowdale and Newlands, especially the Goldscope mine in the latter valley which was exceptionally rich in copper and also yielded lead and silver. Copper ore from Goldscope and the other mines was transported to a new smelter and stamping shed at Brigham in the Greta valley just upstream from the centre of Keswick. Sadly, very little now remains of this once-thriving industrial hamlet, much of which was destroyed in the Civil War.

Keswick's growth was further accelerated by the discovery at Seathwaite in Borrowdale of plumbago (also called wadd, black lead or graphite), which led to the opening of the world's first pencil factory in Keswick in 1566. Local supplies of graphite were finally exhausted in the 1880s, but the Cumberland Pencil Factory's modern works is still in production. Also in Greta Hamlet is the School of Industrial Arts, founded in 1883 by Canon Rawnsley, vicar of Crosthwaite for thirty-four years and a co-founder of the National Trust, to assist men who found work in short supply outside the holiday season. Another contributor to the town's greatly increased prosperity in the sixteenth century was Keswick's woollen industry; early medieval in origin, it was also at its height at this time.

The boom, though, was short-lived; mining activity had slumped by about 1650, and the woollen industry declined to such an extent that by 1800 most of the woollen mills had closed or turned to cotton. In 1749 Keswick was said to be 'greatly decayed and much inferior to what it was formerly'. The town's saviour was the growth of tourism in the nineteenth century, and in particular the arrival of the railway in 1864. The Keswick Hotel was built near the station and by 1900 'Lakes Specials' were running between London Euston and Keswick. Traffic soon declined, however, and now the line has been taken up.

Today Keswick is a typical Lakeland slate town, a rainy day refuge with gift shops, cafés and pubs (many of which sell the excellent draught bitter brewed by Jennings at nearby Cockermouth). Yet there is probably more of interest in this likeable, boisterous town than in some of the tourist traps in southern Lakeland. Starting from St Kentigern's Church, skirt the industrial quarter at Greta Hamlet and, on the left, Greta Hall (home of the poet Robert Southey for forty years) and walk up to the Market Place. Here is the Moot Hall, extravagantly reconstructed in 1813, and, in the alley on the left known as King's Head Yard, is the home of Jonathon Otley, clockmaker turned geologist. There are several of these alleys, including Packhorse Yard and Woolpack Yard, running down from the Market Place towards the River Greta, but the tiny stone-built cottages are now mostly shops or offices.

The parish church of Keswick, St John's, lies beyond the market square. A neat sandstone building with a graceful spire, its main attraction is the view of Derwentwater from its churchyard. More interest lies in the art gallery and museum in Fitz Park, which houses a collection of manuscripts of the Lake Poets (notably an enormous Southey collection), a scale model of the Lake District and some rather odd 'musical stones'. And, finally, there is the Model Railway Exhibition which is housed in the now redundant railway station.

5 SKIDDAW AND BLENCATHRA
Keswick to Threlkeld (13 miles/21km)

Skiddaw dominates the town of Keswick, its great bulk filling the northern horizon and its outliers pressing in on the outskirts of the town. Yet it is often derided, and its virtues are too often thought to be limited to the ease with which it can be climbed and (since the climb is so popular) the improbability of getting lost on the 'tourist' route to its broad summit. But there is much more to the mountain and its subsidiary summits than that; there are excellent and unfrequented ways up from the west and north, crags and waterfalls hidden from the direct route, and a surprising air of tranquillity on the slopes looking out over the desolation of Skiddaw Forest.

The tourist route has its attractions, however, as it rises across the slopes of Latrigg, a flat-topped hill the summit of which was once an open field and is now a favourite belvedere for Derwentwater and the hills framing the lake. Evidence of the route's popularity can be seen in the breadth of the track rising up to Jenkin Hill, past the ruins of the Halfway House, a refreshment hut which once catered for the steady stream of passers-by. There is likely to be further evidence, too, in the form of a trail of litter marking the passage of present day tourists. Nevertheless, this is an easy, although rather unspectacular, way to the summit, and certainly the easiest path to the top of a really high mountain in the Lake District.

A number of quieter and more interesting possibilities present themselves, however. One of the best of these ascends from south of Bassenthwaite by way of the heathery summit of Ullock Pike and the fine ridge of Longside Edge to Carl Side and Skiddaw itself. Unfortunately, transport from Keswick towards Bassenthwaite is necessary and the bus service is rather infrequent, so the recommended Horseshoe route leaves Keswick on foot along Station Street and heads for the bottom of Spooney Green Lane, crossing the bypass on a new bridge and following the tourist route as far as the farm at Thorny Plats. At this point the main track keeps straight on towards Latrigg, but the Horseshoe route bears left and follows the path slanting across a series of fields to Ormathwaite, where the Hall consists of two Georgian houses rather quixotically situated at right angles to each other. Just to the north is Underscar, the Italianate villa of a nineteenth-century Liverpool industrialist.

The field path continues to the hamlet of **Applethwaite**, and now the climbing starts. At first the gradient is gentle and the

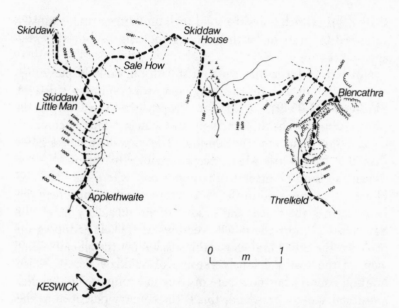

way, along a minor road and then up through a small wood with azaleas and rhododendrons, is full of interest. After leaving the wood further up Applethwaite Gill, however, the slope steepens, and when the route crosses the beck and rises diagonally through the intake to a prominent gate in the wall the climbing becomes a little trying, as it rises through bracken and heather to the right of Grey Crags. Finally, the ridge is reached just north of Jenkin Hill. A left turn here leads to Lesser Man and then to the small grassy platform denoting the top of **Skiddaw Little Man** (2,837ft).

The outlook southwards from Skiddaw Little Man is magnificent, with an uninterrupted view of the main peaks across Derwentwater and Borrowdale. Grasmoor and Eel Crag (with its eastern satellites of Sail, Scar Crags and Causey Pike) are overtopped by High Stile and Pillar; Great Gable and Scafell are seen above Catbells; and to the south-east Helvellyn is viewed in front and to the right of the High Street range. To the north is Skiddaw itself, and the north-eastern horizon is filled by Great Calva and the other rounded fells of Skiddaw Slate country. Where these slates have been eroded, they have tended to leave a shaly debris which hides the solid rock underneath and is usually colonised by grass or heather, giving the fells a subdued, softer appearance.

North from Little Man the tourist path can easily be picked up across a minor col to the long and stony summit ridge of **Skiddaw** (3,053ft), with four tops, the third of them (distinguished from the others by an Ordnance Survey column) being High Man, the true summit. The view here is less good than that from Little Man, except of course to the north, so a return can soon be made to the minor col, where the Lakeland Horseshoe diverges from the tourist path at the point where the latter crosses the fence, and heads for the subsidiary height of **Sale How**. Ignore the raised eyebrows of walkers tramping up or down the broad highway and instead enjoy the all-embracing view of the vast and lonely expanse of Skiddaw Forest. Once hunting country but now bare of trees and composed of heather moor and spongy grassland, this is the country described in the three-day walk around the Back o' Skidda'.

Sale How has practically no features of interest, but the way is fast and easy (although the boggy ground in the slight dip before its rounded, unobtrusive summit can be troublesome) down to **Skiddaw House** and the rough, rutted track – thankfully impassable for cars – from Peter House near Bassenthwaite to Threlkeld. Skiddaw House, instantly recognisable from its windbreak of trees, was once a row of shepherds' cottages, and was also used at one time as a shooting box. It is situated in a splendidly isolated position some three miles from the nearest proper road. The last shepherd left in 1969, but now it has been rescued from dereliction and is used as an outdoor education centre, although one room is available for use as an emergency shelter by the few walkers who pass by this lonely spot.

Leaving Skiddaw House, take the rough track south towards Threlkeld and contour round the prominent spur of Burnt Horse. The track keeps well above the marshy upper valley of the Glenderaterra Beck, but after passing a series of small stone-walled fields the route takes a left fork (the right fork leads round the flank of Lonscale Fell to Keswick) and crosses the stream,

Blencathra
from Castlerigg Stone Circle

then turns left by a sheepfold to climb up by the right bank of
Roughten Gill towards the next objective, Blencathra. This
climb can be postponed for a while, though, by continuing
downstream to the site, just below the confluence of Roughten
Gill with Glenderaterra Beck, of the levels and spoil heaps
associated with a small lead mine, mainly worked early in the
nineteenth century.

The route to Blencathra returns to Roughten Gill and follows
it to its source, the journey brightened by close views of three
small but lively waterfalls. The beck, cascading down past
mountain ashes in a little gorge higher up, is pleasant but the
scenery is unexciting, with the extensive but dull Mungrisdale
Common blotting out most of the northern horizon. The
summit of **Blencathra** (2,847ft) is easily gained up a grassy
slope, with the last few strides revealing the best thing about the
ascent – the sudden, impressive panoramic view southwards of
the High Street range, the northern face of the Helvellyn massif
across the wide Glenderamackin valley, and the central fells
across and to the left of Derwentwater, with the rocky crest of

Gategill Fell forming an effective foreground.

The area around the summit is full of interest. The stony slate debris around the cairn and above the striking ridges on the south face of the mountain was largely formed by the process of periglaciation – frost shattering during the Ice Age, when the lower slopes of Blencathra were blanketed in snow and ice but the upper slopes were exposed to the intense cold – with the result that many of the boulders and smaller stones have been sorted by frost action into stone stripes and, even odder, stone polygons. These roughly circular patterns can be seen, especially during the spring, on the gradual slope north of the summit cairn towards the Saddle, the slight trough between the true summit (Halls Fell Top) and the top of Foule Crag. This grassy trough, especially prominent from the south-east, is responsible for Blencathra's alternative and wholly unattractive name of Saddleback.

Towards the northern end of the Saddle is a white cross laid out in the grass. A memorial to a walker who was killed nearby, the cross consists of stones with a high quartz content, carefully laid out and recently much extended. From the cross, contour above Blue Screes and the crest of Foule Crag, with the infant River Glenderamackin far below, for a dramatic aerial view of Sharp Edge – from here a much more terrifying prospect than Striding Edge from the top of Helvellyn, but in fact a safe and exhilarating walk in good conditions – and Scales Tarn in its dark, deep and steep-sided corrie basin. The edge of the Saddle can now be followed back to the summit cairn, hovering on the brink of the steeply plunging south face of Blencathra.

The southern face of the mountain is dissected by a series of small streams into five main ridges, the central three rocky and narrow towards the summit and separated by valleys which in their upper reaches are wild, steep and worn away to reveal the bare, shattered rock. The contrast between the excitement of this southern face of Blencathra and the tame northern slopes running down to Mungrisdale Common is all the more remarkable since this is the reverse of the usual pattern in the Lake District. The ridges and the deep intervening clefts offer a wide variety of routes of varying degrees of difficulty down to Threlkeld, which lies in the wide valley below. The ravines are probably best used for ascent, and the ridges on each flank, Blease Fell and Scales Fell, give safe but overlong and tedious descents. Probably the best way down for those with some experience of scrambling is the direct route down the central ridge of Halls Fell (the ascent of this is described in the Back o' Skidda' chapter), a scramble down a rocky arête at first, with superlative views on either side down into Doddick Gill and Gate Gill.

A rather easier but still richly rewarding route lies west at first from the summit cairn, then heads down a ribbon of scree onto the upper reaches of Gategill Fell. The ridge, initially on grass, narrows to a rocky arête and beyond this emerges onto the steep fellside above Knott Halloo, a jagged rock tower jutting out into the savage upper valley of Blease Gill. Below Knott Halloo there is nothing to be gained from following the intermittent paths which can be found; instead, plot a course steeply downward through the heather towards Blease Gill, aiming to reach it just below the farm buildings of Blease. The beck can be followed between solid stone walls towards the village of Threlkeld, entering this either down the lane leading to the former Blencathra Sanatorium or, preferably, by keeping to the beck all the way and using a pleasantly sylvan riverside path which emerges near The Horse and Farrier.

Threlkeld enjoyed a brief period of considerable prosperity towards the end of the nineteenth century, when it was quickly transformed from a quiet hamlet into a busy mining village, with up to a hundred men employed at the local mines. The oldest and most important was the lead mine at Gategill, where the 'stope and feather' method of extracting ore (named after the iron implements which were used to break the rock) was in use until blasting with gunpowder was introduced. Together with Woodend mine, lower down the valley of Gate Gill, it was producing five hundred tons of galena a year, and a rather larger quantity of zinc in the 1880s and 1890s. The derelict mine buildings are still standing at Gategill, and unfortunately the spoil heaps lower down the valley are also still with us.

The settlement of Threlkeld has a long history, with the site of a Celtic village (seen during the next stage of the Horseshoe walk) on the northern slopes of Clough Head, and traces of a former open field between the village and the River Glenderamackin. This 'townfield' (the bridge over the river on the Ambleside road is still called Townfield Bridge) covered fourteen acres and at the time of the enclosure award in 1849 consisted of eleven strips, mostly meadowland but with some arable. Today the main source of employment is the large and prominent quarry below Threlkeld Knotts. It yields a blue-grey granite which was previously valued as a building material but is now used only for roadstone.

The village itself, a mixture of cottages, farmsteads, nineteenth-century mineworkers' terraces and more recent speculative development, is now mercifully bypassed by the A66, and to some extent comes to life only with the annual sheepdog trials, a popular tourist attraction held on the third Wednesday in August. The church, dating from 1777, is plain and small and the pubs are more interesting. The Horse and Farrier has an inscription dated 1688 over the door; Wordsworth and De Quincey, during the time Wordsworth was making regular trips on postal business from Grasmere to Penrith, took afternoon tea here every Tuesday. Both The Horse and Farrier and The Salutation still provide good beer, but the former Sun Inn, dating from 1709, now stands forlorn and unvisited on the edge of the village.

6   THE HELVELLYN RANGE
Threlkeld to Patterdale (16 miles/26km)

The sixteen-mile trek along the crest of the Helvellyn massif initially appears daunting but is actually one of the easiest legs of the Lakeland Horseshoe, since much of it consists of a comfortable level walk over gentle grassy slopes, saved from tedium by the superb views down into the deep coves, some separated by narrow, rocky arêtes, on the eastern face of the Helvellyn range.

Indeed one of the most difficult problems of the whole day is how to gain access to the northern foothills from Threlkeld. The ideal route would take the Newsham Farm road and strike up the fellside past the site of the deserted settlement at Threlkeld Knotts in order to reach the Old Coach Road which links Wanthwaite and Dockray; but there is no right of way and it is therefore advisable to trek along the road from Threlkeld to Wanthwaite and take the Old Coach Road from there. This latter route does at least have the merit of climbing the fellside close to the unusually craggy western face of Clough Head, although the Old Coach Road itself seeks out a much gentler gradient, skirting old quarries and rising past a sheepfold (actually named on the map Clough Fold, an indication of the lack of interesting features hereabouts). One feature of great archaeological interest, however, lies only about two hundred yards lower down the fellside to the north. This is the deserted settlement at Threlkeld Knotts.

The remains of the settlement, which is situated on a grassy shelf above the roadstone quarry, looking across the Glenderamackin valley to the striking south face of Blencathra, consist of the boundary walls of a series of roughly rectangular fields and four or five hut circles. Much is obliterated by the heather, but excavation of one of the hut circles showed its walls to be about five feet thick. Below the village site there are quite a number of cairns, associated either with burial or field clearance. The village was perhaps occupied from the first to the eighth century AD, but with its badly drained and north-facing site it is scarcely surprising that it was eventually abandoned in favour of more promising locations.

Back on the Old Coach Road, look out for Hause Well, a spring issuing from well-concealed rocks just south of the track, and at about this point strike up the gentle grassy slope leading to a scattering of rocks at the outlier of White Pike. From here the summit of **Clough Head** (2,382ft) is easily gained. A small wind-shelter and an OS triangulation station mark the highest point, which is the last peak northwards along the Helvellyn ridge and as such has a fine outlook both to the north, to

Blencathra and Skiddaw, and to the south-east, where the central fells form an unusually compact group slightly to the right of the amorphous mass culminating in High Raise.

Helvellyn is still some six miles distant but is approached along a surprisingly level ridge which relies for excitement on the prospect eastwards across rocky ridges to High Street and, later, Ullswater. To the west the upper slopes are broad and convex and the ridge itself offers few challenges at first. Nevertheless there is an opportunity for fast and easy high-level walking, starting with a tramp of about a mile from Clough Head to Calfhow Pike, a small rocky turret marooned in a sea of grass. Down below to the west is the attractive gully containing Sandbed Gill – perhaps the best feature associated with Clough Head – but, sadly, an inspection of this would involve too great a detour from the ridge. Press on instead to the Dodds, a succession of rounded summits along the ridge.

Great Dodd (2,807ft) is the first of these massive fells to be ascended, and it comes as a shock to realise that this tame, grassy summit dome ranks seventeenth in height in the Lake District, higher than, for example, the Langdale Pikes or anything in the High Stile range. Like the rest of the Dodds, it is formed from an extensive lava flow; the lava, on the rare occasions it breaks the surface, is light in colour and columnar in appearance. The cairn is not on the highest point, but makes use of an area of stony ground about a hundred yards north. To the west, broad grassy slopes, occasionally grazed by red deer, descend to Thirlmere, which can be seen from near the cairn. Now a reservoir supplying Manchester, Thirlmere previously consisted of two much smaller natural lakes astride the line of a zone of shattered rock which had succumbed to erosion to form the only major north–south through route in the Lake District.

A broad, flat-topped ridge now leads around the head of Mill Gill to **Watson's Dodd** (2,584ft), which boasts as its main contribution to Lake District scenery, again well away from the ridge, the Castle Rock of Triermain, now an important rock-climbing crag but previously noted as the setting for Sir Walter Scott's 'The Bridal of Triermain'. The walk continues past a

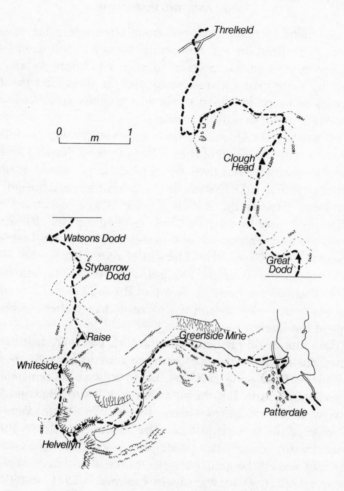

diminutive pool to the top of **Stybarrow Dodd** (2,770ft). To the west is the attractive valley of Stanah Gill, with its waterfalls and deeply scoured ravine. On the ridge itself there is little of interest during the comfortable descent to Sticks Pass.

At 2,420ft Sticks Pass is the second highest pass in the Lake District (only Esk Hause is higher). The pass coincides with a band of faulted rock, and copper veins associated with the faulting have intermittently been worked in the area. The name is derived from the posts, long since vanished, driven into the ground to mark the line of the track which was used by packhorse trains carrying lead ore from Greenside mine to the smelters at Brigham and Stonycroft. Nowadays the track, the ancient route from Glenridding to Stanah and once so busy, is nothing more than a narrow stony path in places, and the dull scenery and eerie loneliness of the spot combine to make Sticks Pass seem curiously unwelcoming.

Fortunately the Horseshoe route now enters more promising territory with the ascent of the northern flanks of Raise, a hive of activity in winter since these slopes retain snow as long as most in the area. The Lake District Ski Club has a hut perched on the north-east slope at the 2,500ft contour. Close to this are the relics of a mile-long stone flue, running up the fell from Greenside mine to the site of a chimney in use when lead was smelted on the spot (the Horseshoe route passes the mine buildings in due course). The grassy slopes leading up from Sticks Pass become stony as the top of **Raise** (2,889ft) is neared, and the neat, rocky summit is a pleasant change after the bland tops of the Dodds.

The route is still predominantly on turf, however, as it leaves Raise and heads south-west for more than half a mile to the summit of **Whiteside** (2,832ft), noted only for its remarkably large summit cairn. But the views are now improving considerably, with the line of crags above Keppel Cove encroaching to the edge of the summit plateau. The former Keppelcove Tarn, now a marshy hollow, was previously a reservoir for the Greenside lead mine; the tarn burst its banks after heavy rain in October 1927, the dam was further breached in 1931, and it has never been repaired. The 1927 disaster led to floods in Glenridding as the water rushed down the valley, drowning animals, destroying bridges and wrecking a number of buildings. Above the former Keppelcove Tarn is Brown Cove Tarn, which was itself an earlier reservoir supplying the mine and was then much larger. The green, flat, marshy land around the tarn and the ruined buildings testify to its former importance.

A well-cairned path leads south from Whiteside to Helvellyn Lower Man, but in clear weather the cairns are hardly necessary: the path is clearly visible leading towards the next summit with, to its left, the top of Helvellyn itself above its superb eastern ridges of Swirral Edge and Striding Edge. There is now a depressingly substantial descent to a grassy col above Brown Cove, and then a steady and stony climb to Lower Man (3,033ft), an outlier of Helvellyn rather than a truly separate summit. The ridge changes direction here, now trending south-east around the edge of Water Crag and above the top of Swirral Edge to reach the summit of Helvellyn.

Helvellyn (3,118ft) is perhaps the most attractive of the Lakeland Threethousanders in the eyes of the average walker – the Scafells are too 'difficult', Skiddaw lacks dramatic appeal – and it has paid the full penalty for its magnetic attraction. The Brathay Exploration Group counted 614 visitors on its summit on a wet Tuesday in July 1966, and it is highly unlikely that the number of people reaching the top on any day during the summer is any less now. The litter and the state of the paths argue precisely the opposite. Yet the odd thing is that the fourteen routes converging on its summit reach a peak which, except to the east where there is a magnificent view down into the corrie containing Red Tarn, in a steep-sided basin between two arêtes, is broad, grassy and of no great intrinsic interest, despite the presence of a small summit cairn, a wall-shelter, an OS pillar, a couple of monuments – one commemorating the landing of an aeroplane in 1926 and the other (the Gough Memorial) a devoted dog who stayed with his dead master in 1885 – and sundry unnecessary cairns.

There is a choice of routes from Helvellyn to journey's end at Patterdale. Many will wish to traverse Striding Edge, but this is a popular and often overcrowded route, badly worn in places, and the descent by Swirral Edge and Red Tarn Beck is recommended as a quieter alternative. (For those who must try Striding Edge, however, it is possible to follow the arête – which Harry Griffin has called 'one of the most spectacular mountain walks in the Lake District' and calls for some rock scrambling, though the romantic view of Striding Edge as a place of terror is greatly exaggerated – to the wall at the end of Birkhouse Moor and then bear left, over the stile, to reach the path descending by

Helvellyn, Swirral Edge and Red Tarn

Red Tarn Beck.) The way down to Swirral Edge from the top of Helvellyn lies past the OS column and a prominent cairn, and then excitingly down on bare rock with Red Tarn far below on the right and the pyramid peak of Catstycam directly ahead. Beyond the rocks the path leaves the ridge and veers down towards the outlet of the tarn.

Red Tarn is so superbly situated that it seems incredible that so few people visit its shores. Cradled between the savage rock ridges of Striding Edge and Swirral Edge, and with an almost vertical back wall rising 800ft to the summit of Helvellyn, it adorns one of the finest corries in the Lake District. The low dam constructed in the 1860s to raise the water level and so convert it into a reservoir (yet another serving the lead mine at Greenside) seems out of place, although it was only when the mine was closed in 1962 that this particular use was abandoned. An oddity of Red Tarn is that it is the only tarn stocked with schelly, a kind of freshwater herring which is a relic of the Ice Age and is found only here and in Ullswater.

The way down to Glenridding and Patterdale follows the northern bank of Red Tarn Beck for its entire course. At first it crosses peat hags, and later some sections are very wet, a fact which becomes depressingly obvious from the vivid green hues of the vegetation. Later the path drops more steeply as the confluence of Red Tarn Beck with Glenridding Beck is approached, and a new causeway and footbridge have to be negotiated. A well-graded path follows Glenridding Beck, which flows through an attractive ravine with rowan trees clinging to the sheer sides, to the less attractive surroundings of Greenside mine.

At its zenith **Greenside** was the most important lead mine in the district. The lead vein was discovered in the seventeenth century, although it was not until 1822 that the Greenside Mining Company was formed. The early success of the company was astounding: the shares increased tenfold in value in ten years. The total profit from the 250,000 tons of lead concentrates raised at the mine has been calculated at about £400,000, although this could well be a gross underestimation. At first the ore was carried across Sticks Pass for smelting, but as production increased it was sent to a more modern smelter at Alston Moor. In 1830 a smelter was constructed at Greenside itself, but this eventually proved to be uneconomic and the ore was carted to Troutbeck station and sent by rail to Newcastle. The storm in 1927 which wrecked the dam and unleashed the waters of Keppelcove Tarn on Glenridding almost sank the mining company, which had to pay compensation, and the depression of the 1930s did halt production. Work restarted, however, after a few years and continued until the deposits were worked out and the mine was closed for good in 1962.

Now the mine is closed, the full effects of its devastation of the environment can be seen all too clearly. Despite considerable attempts to devise a method of grassing (and thereby disguising) the spoil heaps, they are painfully obvious to travellers alongside Glenridding Beck. The mine buildings have been tidied up (one by the YHA) but they still represent an intrusion into the valley, and upstream the evidence of dereliction and decay is even more marked. So a venture which brought much-needed employment, and dominated Glenridding to the extent that the mining

by Ullswater

company owned more than fifty of the terraced cottages in the village, is now notable only as a despoiler of the landscape.

From the mine take the well-graded and expertly constructed track on the southern side of Glenridding Beck and contour round the lower slopes of Birkhouse Moor (there are fine views across Ullswater from a little higher up), gradually diverging from the beck, before bearing left down to Gillside Farm, then past a camp site and alongside the beck to join a substantial track leading to the main road at Glenridding. Patterdale lies about a mile to the south along the A592; there is no alternative to using the road (which does have a footpath for most of the way), although those with the energy to visit Glenridding Pier can keep to the shore of Ullswater, with views across to Place Fell, for part of the way.

Patterdale is little more than a hamlet strung out along the main road at the head of the lake, with a couple of hotels and not a great deal else. Now famous chiefly for its sheepdog trials, held on 'Dogs Day' on the last Saturday in August, it has for some time relied mainly on tourists for its survival. The medieval chapel of St Patrick was rebuilt in 1853, and St Patrick's Well, by the roadside north of the village, was once reputed to have healing properties but is now housed in an incongruous gabled stone recess. The focus of interest in Patterdale, described by H. H. Symonds in 1933 in his *Walking in the Lake District* as 'a most unlovely place, made of buses and booths and scrappy bits of architectural jumble', is its superb situation at the head of Ullswater and surrounded by high fells.

7 HIGH STREET
Patterdale to Troutbeck (13 miles/21km)

The Lakeland Horseshoe heads south along the main road from the Patterdale Hotel, turns left after about two hundred yards, crosses Goldrill Bridge and the valley flat of Goldrill Beck past Placefell House, then bears left along a minor road and quickly turns right, following the slate signpost to Boredale Hause and Angle Tarn. Through a gate and onto the open fell, the path begins to climb steeply upwards to the right, with Patterdale, Ullswater and Striding Edge increasingly lovely in retrospect. At a junction of paths the direct way to Angle Tarn keeps right, but the higher path to the left can be followed backbreakingly upwards through the bracken to Boredale Hause.

The hause is a confusing maze of marshy paths, and regrettably there are few remaining signs of the Chapel in the Hause, a medieval chapel established in this isolated spot to serve the small community of Boredalehead. Only a handful of carved stones are left to indicate that the highest limits of settlement are now a good deal lower than they were in the fifteenth century. William Wordsworth describes his visit to the ruins in his *Guide to the Lakes*: 'Scarcely did the Druids, when they fled to these fastnesses, perform their rites in any situation more exposed to disturbance from the elements . . . What dismal storms must have often drowned the voice of the preacher!'

It is worth digressing north-east to look down into the deserted, peaceful trough of Boredale, named after the wild boar, a woodland animal which seems to have died out by the thirteenth century as the forests gave way to sheep pastures. But

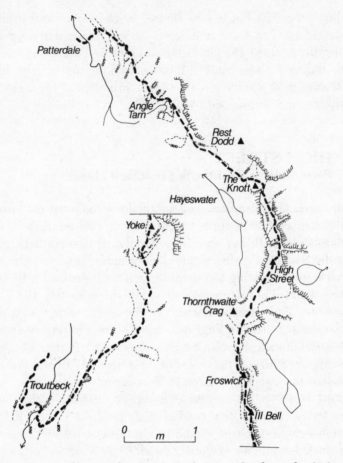

the main route lies south across rough ground, after a final glance back to the head of Ullswater, above Rake Crag and round the deeply incised headwaters of Dubhow Beck, with Deepdale and Dovedale prominent across Brothers Water. The rocky tor crowning the first of the two turrets of Angletarn Pikes lies ahead, and can easily be visited by means of a short scramble, although the main path keeps to the right of the pikes and swings round a corner to burst upon the scene of **Angle Tarn**, a shallow ridge tarn formed by the deposition of lateral moraine. Its diminutive islands, rocky headlands and reed-choked southern fringes are backed by the High Street massif.

The path gradually makes its way around the tarn, becoming very muddy at times, to reach the eastern shore from where there is an extraordinary prospect across the water of the Fairfield fells and, on the other side of Grisedale, Helvellyn and Catstycam overtopping Striding Edge. Beyond Angle Tarn the route climbs steadily below Buck Crag, with Hayeswater coming into view on the right, and passes through a gate at a junction of walls. Keeping the wall on the right, the path weaves between rocky hillocks to Satura Crag, which looks out over the length of the remote, glaciated valley of Bannerdale, its upper reaches now deserted but once the site of a prehistoric settlement. The highest farm now, Dale Head, is more than a mile and a half down the valley from the steep scree slopes below Satura Crag; a typical statesman farm, it was rebuilt in the seventeenth century and still has the foundations of a former spinning gallery.

Over on the other side of the ridge, below **Hayeswater**, which now functions as a reservoir for Penrith, is some rather more substantial evidence of this architectural style in the hamlet of Low Hartsop. Lying slightly away from the main road, Low Hartsop has until recently survived the impact of tourism well, and two spinning galleries survive, that at Mireside being an outstanding example of this local architectural tradition. The hamlet was described as 'decaying' by Wordsworth, and now only two working farms are left; many of the other dwellings are occupied as second homes. There is decay, too, around the village. The ruinous foundations of the corn mill, worked as recently as 1913, lie upstream, and derelict hogg-houses (winter shelters for yearling sheep) and invading bracken in the intake fields point to changes in agricultural practice.

The next section of the Lakeland Horseshoe, from Satura Crag to The Knott, is the most trying of the day, with progress across the unappealing lower slopes of **Rest Dodd** (2,278ft) hampered by very wet ground which, in the vicinity of the many small streams, turns all too readily into a peaty morass. The scenery at this stage is also rather tame, enlivened only by the panorama of the Fairfield range across the humpy glacial moraine around Hayeswater. Even when the largest of these streams is crossed

The Knott and Straits of Riggindale

and the slope steepens, peat hags and areas of marshy ground continue to cause diversions, and it is with some relief that a prominent cairn on the side of The Knott is reached and the route swings left up a rutted track to reach the col between Rampsgill Head and The Knott.

A minor diversion to the left at this point, towards the striking crags forming the north-west face of Rampsgill Head, reaches a spot which looks out along the Rampsgill valley and over the Martindale deer forest. This medieval deer sanctuary is solidly defended in strategic places by barbed wire and 'Keep Out' notices (The Nab is virtually a forbidden hill for walkers, although it is fair to say that it would not attract many if access were unrestricted) and now consists of bare, treeless slopes, although two patches of relict woodland high above Rampsgill Beck are a reminder of the once extensive forest cover. Back on the main route, the way to the summit of **The Knott** (2,423ft) lies past the pale blue mountain rescue hut, although there will be a temptation to omit the short but dull trudge to the undistinguished top. A fine peak when seen from Hayeswater, The Knott from here is simply a slight rise on the end of a spur.

Once past this point, the highlights of the walk are at hand as the main High Street ridge is gained at the Straits of Riggindale, the narrowest part of this long, straight mountain range. The Straits were formed by the glacial erosion of corries on either side of the ridge. Look back northwards from just above the Straits to see the main ridge twisting right towards Rampsgill Head and High Raise, and the subsidiary spur leading off on the left towards The Knott and Rest Dodd. A choice of routes is available up the gentle northern slopes of High Street itself: furthest to the west is the line of the Roman road from Brocavum near Penrith to the fort of Galava at the head of Windermere (this is the route followed in the Roman Way); in the centre is the wall which traverses the ridge and provides a useful guide in mist; while to the east a route following the rim of the crags falling towards Riggindale can boast the most impressive scenery.

The deep bowl of Riggindale, a classic example of a U-shaped glaciated valley, and the fine narrow ridge of Long Stile, cradling at its foot a small pool in the hollow of Caspel Gate, form an eerie picture in mist, with the shadowy outline of Haweswater in the middle distance. Indeed, as the top of High Street slowly comes into view, it becomes apparent that the approach from Rough Crag and Long Stile (used by the Hidden Valleys walk) is the only really satisfactory way to climb the mountain, which is grassy and rounded in all directions except to the east. From the white cairn at the top of Long Stile, the Ordnance Survey column marking the top of **High Street** (2,718ft) can be seen across a waste of tussocky grass and peat hags. The view from the column, close to the wall, is extensive but not particularly attractive, and the outlook is generally more pleasing from the edges of the large and flat summit plateau, where the interplay between mountain and lake enhances the scene.

The nature of the summit plateau had its compensations not only for the Romans, who found it a quick, direct and trouble-free route across the eastern Lake District, but also for later generations of Cumbrians who held an annual shepherds' meet and fair day here until 1835. Barrels of beer were rolled up from Mardale, and wrestling and even horse-racing took place (the summit is still called Racecourse Hill on Ordnance Survey maps). But there are few natural attractions on this vast sheepwalk to delay the walker, who can quickly set off south-west, following the wall and then curving round to the right to reach the summit of **Thornthwaite Crag** (2,569ft). The chances of going astray here are negligible, for the highest point is spectacularly celebrated by a slender and distinctive 14ft pillar, elegantly constructed on a small rock outcrop.

Thornthwaite Crag can also boast a finer view from its summit than that from High Street, with the fine ridge of Froswick and Ill Bell separating the valleys of Kentmere and Troutbeck, and the long finger of Windermere in the distance. Round to the west Scafell and Scafell Pike can be picked out, fifteen miles away, in the clearest weather, and to the north-west lies the Helvellyn range, with Skiddaw and Blencathra behind. The route lies south, however, back to the main ridge and then sticks to the ridge top, heading for Ill Bell and the Garburn Pass, when the Roman road bears right to descend to Troutbeck (this route, described as part of the Roman Way, can be used if time is short or energy sapped by the long ascent of High Street).

The ascent of the first peak, **Froswick** (2,359ft), is perfectly straightforward. The grassy ridge leads directly to the summit, with the wild head of Kentmere and Kentmere Reservoir below the jagged profile of Froswick's craggy eastern slopes. The small summit area is pleasantly rocky; away to the north can be seen the deep gash of Threshthwaite Mouth and the beacon crowning Thornthwaite Crag. The ridge continues easily south on excellent turf to the col above Over Cove, then climbs steadily up to **Ill Bell** (2,476ft), the highest and most graceful of the trio of peaks on this ridge. There is a classic prospect of Windermere from the summit, which is liberally adorned with cairns, and from the edge of the crags just to the east Kentmere Reservoir is prominent.

The quality of the walk is maintained as far as the summit of **Yoke** (2,309ft), an unassuming peak, by keeping to the edge of the crags around Rainsborrow Cove. The western slopes of Yoke are tedious, but to the east is the precipice of Rainsborrow

Crag. The summit plateau is a compromise between the two, with a lot of grass but some outcrops of rock, one of which forms the foundation for the summit cairn. The way down to the top of the Garburn Pass picks up the wall leading southwards to a very small tarn, then bears rather to the right, aiming to avoid as much as possible of the marshy ground lower down. Even the driest route will, however, encounter some pretty wet ground on the lower parts of the broad, peaty ridge just before the Garburn road is reached.

The Garburn Pass is the natural through route between Troutbeck and Kentmere, following the line of a thin band of Coniston Limestone which has stood up less well to the ravages of time than the harder volcanic rocks to the north and Silurian shales further south. In a westerly direction the Garburn road, formerly an important packhorse route but now a lonely, rutted and very stony track, very gradually approaches Troutbeck. The approach is infuriatingly slow, and for once a steeper and more direct route would be preferable to the desperately gentle descent in which the road at times appears to be travelling parallel to the valley road through Troutbeck rather than getting any closer to the village.

Eventually the Garburn road, by now a walled and eroded lane, reaches the church at **Troutbeck** via a zigzag path by The Howe. The church, with three lych gates, was built on the site of an earlier chapel in 1736 and was restored in 1831; its outstanding feature is the stained glass in the east window, a good example of the style of Burne-Jones and Morris. The village street, which straggles along for a mile on a shelf above the Trout Beck valley, should be tackled from south to north, which has the advantage of starting at the magnificent seventeenth-century farmhouse of Town End and finishing in the bar of The Queen's Head at Town Head.

Town End, the farmhouse of the Browne family, was built in 1623 (the family had lived in a previous house on the same site for about a hundred years). The Brownes continued to live there until 1943, and shortly afterwards it became the property of the National Trust, so that an early example of a statesman's farmhouse, with a marvellously authentic interior, remains intact. The central portion of the house is the oldest, and the cylindrical chimneys, slate roof and mullioned windows are all typical of the Westmorland style of building. Inside, many original domestic items, including an old-fashioned cheese press, a mangle and a wooden washing machine, have been retained.

Opposite Town End is an excellent example, dated 1666, of a bank barn, a type of barn peculiar to the Yorkshire Dales and the Lake Counties, and in the next mile north there are well over a dozen seventeenth- and eighteenth-century statesman farms, although one or two are ruinous and others have been converted into twentieth-century residences and altered almost beyond recognition. An interesting feature of Troutbeck is the way that the farms and cottages are clustered together at certain points, so that even today there is no focal point to the village. At the same time each of the clusters is connected to the others by a bewilderingly complex network of lanes, tracks and field paths. A close study of the map reveals the reason for these clusters: each occurs close to one or more wells (often named on the map) from which communal water supplies were obtained.

The cluster of dwellings at Town Head, quite distinct from the rest of the village, includes The Queen's Head Inn, an ancient hostelry with real ale, slab floors and a throne in the Mayor's Parlour, which since 1779 has been the scene of the annual mayor-making ceremony. Nowadays the mayor's only duties are to organise the annual hunt and name his successor, but previously his most important function was to act as mediator in any disputes which arose in the village. On a fine evening, the tables outside The Queen's Head provide a suitable final objective for the Lakeland Horseshoe. An alternative finish avoids Troutbeck and continues southwards above Longmire, using a series of lanes and paths to reach Far Orrest, Crosses, Elleray Bank (an easy diversion to the left leads to Orrest Head, renowned as a viewpoint for Windermere and the Langdale Pikes), and finally Windermere town, virtually next to the railway station. This is a disappointing end to such a fine excursion, however, and the exploration of Troutbeck is a much more fitting conclusion.

BACK O' SKIDDA'

Many visitors to the Lake District will know the southern slopes, if not the summits, of Skiddaw and Blencathra; few indeed will have ventured further north onto the very different slopes of the Uldale and Caldbeck fells. Yet the country known as Back o' Skidda' can provide exhilarating walking well away from the crowds. Strong walkers will possibly consider completing the circuit in two days, with an overnight break in Keswick.

1 THE CALDBECK AND ULDALE FELLS
Mungrisdale to Bassenthwaite (12 miles/19km)

The starting point for the first day's walk is the attractive and remarkably unspoilt village of **Mungrisdale**, a settlement split into two parts, one straggling along the valley of the River Glenderamackin at the point where it emerges from the hills and turns sharply south, and the other huddling below Raven Crags, the stern eastern face of Bowscale Fell. The small whitewashed church, one of a number in the area dedicated to St Kentigern (also known as St Mungo, hence the name of the village), has a three-decker pulpit but is otherwise undistinguished.

The route lies past the former village school, now the post office, taking the fell road north to Mosedale past the substantial farm of Undercrag. As the brooding cluster of farm buildings at Bowscale is approached, the steep southern slopes of Carrock Fell, soon to be climbed, take on an increasingly precipitous appearance. The fell, a geological oddity, is a complete contrast to its neighbours in this lonely territory behind Blencathra and

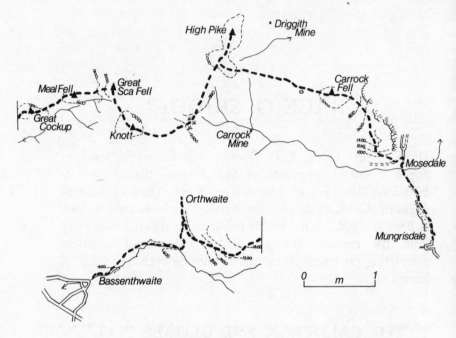

Skiddaw. Volcanic gabbro and granophyre intruded by faulting has resulted in a rocky mountain, with a wall of crags facing east, in the midst of the smooth, slaty fells all around.

Cross Mosedale Bridge – either the attractive but now redundant old one or its twentieth-century replacement – and look upstream along the deeply incised course of the Caldew, a small stream but one which has carved its valley deeply back into the rounded fells. Turn left at the junction of roads opposite the car park in the hamlet of **Mosedale**, which is little more than a handful of slate cottages beneath Carrock Fell. This road (which leads to Carrock mine) can be left at a number of points before, opposite or just after the last cottages. There is no real merit in following any particular route up the excruciatingly steep fellside, since all of them encounter a band of steep, loose rock mixed with heather and gorse. Higher up, as is usual with Lakeland fells, the slope eases, and eventually a bouldery plateau with burnt heather and bilberry, interspersed with marshy patches, is reached.

Perspiring walkers will be dismayed on reaching the plateau to discover that the top of Carrock Fell is still a considerable distance away across very uneven ground, but the ascent is well worth while. On the way there is an extensive view to the right across the Eden valley, and on the approach to the summit from the south-east the route passes through the surprisingly substantial remains of a hill fort. The walls still stand to a height of three or four feet in places, and gaps denoting gateways or, possibly, the slighting of the fort by the Romans, are also plainly visible. The cairn marking the summit of **Carrock Fell** (2,174ft) lies within the hill fort and is attended by a particularly well-constructed and efficient wind-shelter.

The hill fort on Carrock Fell covers about five acres and is the largest known example in Cumbria. There are no signs of foundations of hut circles inside the fort, although at the east end there is a cairn with traces of a cist at its centre, and indeed the fort is difficult to date, though it was presumably in use in the Iron Age. The extra gaps in the walls, together with the heap of rubble at the south-west corner, near a sheepfold, have been interpreted as evidence that the fort was dismantled by the Romans when they assumed control of the area in the first century AD. Whatever its history, this fort on the top of the unusually rocky Carrock Fell was magnificently sited, crowning the last major summit of the Lakeland fells to the north-east and towering above a steep and craggy descent to the Caldew plain.

Leave the summit cairn and pass through the fort's western gateway, heading for High Pike, which is very much in view but lies beyond the wide and boggy shoulder of Carrock Fell. A path exists in places, but is sometimes elusive and in any case is little drier than any other route leading to the unimportant hump of Miton Hill. To the left of the ridge, across the deep Caldew valley, is the dark corrie containing Bowscale Tarn, backed by its parent fell and, further into the distance, Blencathra and Skiddaw. The head of the Caldew can be seen to the south-west and the conspicuous dark-green foliage of the Skiddaw House windbreak can be easily identified. On the northern side of the ridge the entrance to **Driggith Mine**, worked in the early nine-

Carrock Fell
and Skiddaw Forest

teenth century, is prominent in a gully on the flank of High Pike. In 1820 about forty men were employed here, and the mine was prolific enough for a smelter and stamping mill to be built lower down the Carrock Beck; yet by 1870 the mine had been abandoned. The gullies running down to Drygill Beck are also noteworthy. Steep-sided and severely eroded, stripped bare of all vegetation, such gullies are common on the Caldbeck Fells and appear curiously out of place on these otherwise smooth and grassy slopes.

The section from Miton Hill to the col between High Pike and Great Lingy Hill is on bleached tussocky grass and is wet in places (the name Drygill Head on the large-scale maps is distinctly inappropriate here), but there is some improvement as a track is crossed and the summit of **High Pike** (2,157ft) is approached. High Pike is the most northerly peak of over two thousand feet in the Lake District, and the bizarre collection of man-made objects surrounding the highest point seems to be some sort of celebration of this fact. Apart from the cairn, an OS column and a squat wind-shelter, there is a slate seat (a memorial to a local man), a bare patch surrounded by turf which is the site of Caldbeck's beacon on special occasions, and the disintegrating ruins of a shepherd's cottage. The net effect of this clutter is to emphasise the fine views north and east across the Caldew valley, and south to Sharp Edge on Blencathra.

Head back across the grassy slopes of High Pike to the track coming up from Calebrack and follow this over the flank of Great Lingy Hill (the summit is an easy diversion over the heather which gives the fell its name, but is hardly worth while) to the bothy at the head of the Grainsgill Beck valley. Much of the surrounding area was maintained until shortly after the Second World War as a grouse moor, and this hut, together with various shooting butts and hides scattered around the fellsides, is a relic of that era. More recently it has acted as an emergency shelter offering rudimentary but effective accommodation for anyone unfortunate enough to get into difficulties in the desolate wastes behind Skiddaw. It has often fallen into disrepair and yet been reprieved; on my last visit a notice by the visitor's book explained that 'this hut was due to be demolished, but repairs in August 1982 may keep it habitable a little longer – please do not damage it.' The visitor's book was surprisingly full: about forty names had been added in the previous month.

From the bothy the buildings around **Carrock Mine**, lower down Grainsgill Beck, are visible. Not begun until 1854, and then not very successfully, the mine came into its own in the First World War, when the Carrock Mining Syndicate was extracting tungsten ores (wolfram and scheelite) from quartz veins in the Skiddaw granite. The slump in the price of tungsten in 1919 led to the cessation of activity and more recent working of the mine has been sporadic, the last explorations taking place in the early 1970s. Over twenty minerals have been identified in the vicinity of the mine, and summer weekends often see amateur geologists collecting specimens.

A more surprising enterprise, over on the northern face of Great Lingy Hill, was the Caldbeck china clay mine. The workings were situated at about 1,800ft, below Hare Stones;

yet, despite the remote and exposed situation of the mine, several
hundred tons of china clay were brought to the surface before the
operation ceased. Great Lingy Hill's final curiosity is the
appalling morass of Miller Moss, the collecting ground for
Grainsgill Beck. The crossing of the beck can be desperately
difficult even after a period of dry weather, with heathery swamp
and shallow pools of water presenting formidable obstacles.

The north-eastern slopes of Knott are also fairly damp initially,
but eventually the gradient becomes more gentle and the route
traverses the featureless grass prairie surrounding the summit of
Knott (2,329ft), the highest of the fells at the Back o' Skidda',
but also one of the dullest. On the way to the summit cairn,
rarely visited and consisting of just a handful of stones, is the one
redeeming feature – the glimpse southwards through the narrow
wedge separating Blencathra and Skiddaw of the highest fells in
the Lake District. Just to the right of this cleft is the attractive
pyramid peak of Great Calva.

The summit plateau is so broad and so flat that the easiest way
to approach the next objective, Great Sca Fell, is to take a
compass bearing (north-west) and head across the turf down to
the col between the two fells. The col is defended by a series of
peat hags which are difficult to avoid and unpleasant in wet
weather, but there are no other problems in the three-quarters of
a mile from Knott to the top of **Great Sca Fell** (2,131ft), the
focal point of the gentle, grassy Uldale fells. The view from the
extensive summit sheepwalk is of no great interest, being largely
confined to nearby fells, although Bassenthwaite Lake is now in
sight away to the west.

The last two summits are now close at hand, and are quickly
reached across excellent turf. Head west down the fellside, with
the deep ravine of Frozenfell Gill below on the left, and then
climb the tussocky grass slope to the prominent, and at times
very welcome, wind-shelter on the exposed and pleasantly intricate summit of **Meal Fell** (1,770ft). Two rocky humps are
separated by a marshy depression containing two or three small
pools; the scene, and especially the naked rock, seems quite
foreign to the Uldale fells. The final peak, Great Cockup, is of

even more modest proportions, but is separated from Meal Fell by the remarkable gash of Trusmadoor. A few bare rocks decorate the steeply plunging upper slopes on either side of the 'pass', and the lower slopes, consisting mostly of precariously balanced slaty scree, are awkward to negotiate, yet the bottom is green and smooth, and indeed lies only just above the Burntod Gill valley. The explanation appears to be that Trusmadoor formed a small glacial overflow channel, its steep sides and flat bottom gouged out by moving ice.

From the bottom of Trusmadoor the first stage of the climb up to Great Cockup appears somewhat forbidding, on scree and then on steep, slippery grass. It can be avoided on either side, but only at some cost in time and distance and loss of face. Above the rocks the going becomes much easier as the flat, heather-covered summit area of **Great Cockup** (1,720ft) is gained. Ahead is the outlying fell of Binsey, with Bassenthwaite Lake to its left. Further left lies Skiddaw, fronted by the dark bowl of Dead Crags. The view left improves as the south-west slopes of Great Cockup are tackled and Dash Farm, with its windbreak of trees, and the cascades of Whitewater Dash come into view.

These south-west slopes of Great Cockup were once a ling-covered grouse moor, but now that they are used only for grazing the amount of heather has dwindled rapidly and what remains is untidy and deteriorating. The resultant grassy slope can be followed down to a prominent boulder – a fine viewpoint for Whitewater Dash – and then to a bridleway running through the bracken on the lower slopes. Turn right along this green track and follow it to the rough farm road running below Orthwaite Bank. Where this joins a surfaced road at an acute angle, continue north for a quarter of a mile to reach the moorland hamlet of **Orthwaite**, a quiet farming community above the small lake of Over Water. The seventeenth-century hall is of some architectural interest, and there is a surprisingly rich set of archaeological finds in the vicinity, with an earthwork behind the hall (the hillock overlooking the hamlet is called Castle How) and a moated enclosure close to the track leading to Overwater Hall.

Two routes to Bassenthwaite are now feasible. The more straightforward leads back along the fell road for half a mile before turning right just before Cassbeck Bridge to follow a quiet lane through a miniature gorge, with the cascading Halls Beck on the left and Whitefield Wood on the right. The wood, at first consisting mostly of silver birch amongst rocky outcrops, is particularly pleasant. Later a more standardised Forestry Commission treescape spreads to both sides of the road as Park Wood is entered and the alternative route from Orthwaite joins from the right.

This second route has the merit of avoiding roads as far as possible, but lies on little-used paths across farmland in part and is not too easy to follow. Take the footpath on the left just to the north of Orthwaite Farm and bear left after 200 yards to cross the River Ellen a short distance below Little Tarn, a small and reedy pool in a shallow valley. At a junction of paths continue straight ahead (roughly south-west) across a spur above White-field Wood, cross the headwaters of a minor stream and slant steeply down through Park Wood to reach the minor road described above. The two routes now follow the lane into the village of **Bassenthwaite**, which is first glimpsed across the fields as the view opens out and the conifers retreat to the top of the slope on the right. The village is reached over a substantial bridge near The Sun Inn, at the end of a surprisingly varied and almost certainly uncrowded day in the far northern fells.

2   SKIDDAW FROM THE NORTH
Bassenthwaite to Threlkeld (9 miles/14km)

The centre of the compact village of **Bassenthwaite** lies well away from the lake of the same name, although this has not always been the case. Two miles south of the village, down an unmade track and close to the lake shore, is the church of St Bega. The chancel arch is Norman and there are traces of thirteenth-century work, but overall the impression is of an over-zealous Victorian restoration. The newer church of St John, built

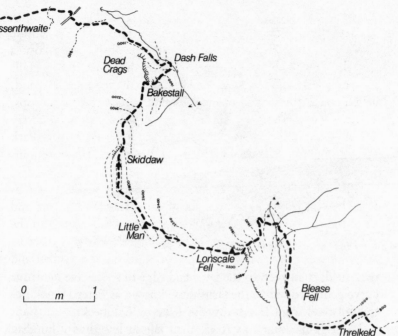

in 1878 in a rather elaborate style, also stands aloof from the village and, together with the village school and a few houses, forms the hamlet of Chapel. The core of the village is the informal, irregularly shaped green, with a comfortable mixture of older slate-grey cottages and newer housing leading down to the stream. At the top end of the settlement is the village pub and a disused mill.

The main objective of the day's walk is the ascent of Skiddaw, which fills much of the southern horizon with its vast bulk. Several possibilities present themselves, but the most interesting line of approach takes in a visit to Dash Falls (Whitewater Dash on most maps) and then skirts the dark rim of Dead Crags before reaching Bakestall, the ridge of Broad End and finally the long, bouldery summit ridge of Skiddaw. The route leaves Bassenthwaite by taking the lane, which quickly becomes a field path, leading eastwards from the village green. Keep parallel to, but some way above, Halls Beck to begin with, but after crossing two fields take the right-hand path and cut diagonally across the

Whitewater Dash,
Dead Crags and Skiddaw

next field, then keep to the left-hand edge of successive fields and curve gently round to the farmhouse known as Peter House, and the fell road from Bassenthwaite Lake to Caldbeck.

Turn right along this road, then left in less than a hundred yards onto the gated road leading to Skiddaw House. This well-known track, fortunately unfit for cars, forms a through route to Threlkeld (and can be followed throughout its length if the weather rules out the climb to the top of Skiddaw). The track meanders pleasantly along the side of the Dash valley, with the road to Dash Farm dropping down to the left after about three-quarters of a mile. The waterfalls at Whitewater Dash are now in view, and after Dead Beck is forded the pastoral greens of the Dash valley give way to the gaunt grey cliffs of Dead Crags, with a strange mixture of fierce rock and loose scree in a great eerie hollow. The Skiddaw House road can be seen gently rising ahead, and this is followed to the base of the rock step which has led to the formation of Whitewater Dash.

The scene around Whitewater Dash is attractive enough from the road, but the real excitement of this tremendous series of falls can only be sensed from the foot of the little gorge, which can easily be reached. Samuel Taylor Coleridge, on one of his lonely pilgrimages across the fells from Keswick, saw **Dash Falls** on an

October day in 1800, and considered them 'more completely atomised and white than any other I have seen . . . they are the finest water furies I ever beheld'. So this sinuous series of steep rapids careering over the rock step at the head of the Dash valley helps give the lie to the popular myth that Back o' Skidda' country is desolate and uninteresting.

Above Dash Falls the route leaves the lonely track to Skiddaw House – still more than a mile away in its astonishingly isolated position at the head of the Caldew valley – and climbs up by a wall before inclining over to the right to ascend Birkett Edge as close as possible to the rim of **Dead Crags**. The cliffs on the far side of the curving line of crags stand out impressively in front of the outlying fell of Binsey (formed of Borrowdale Volcanic rocks which have somehow been misplaced in a sea of softer surrounding rocks), and the foreground is filled by the craggy hollow below the cliffs, a jumble of little arêtes, solid buttresses and heather and bilberry hollows. Rock climbers have found little of interest in Dead Crags, largely because the rock is unreliable and too broken up by vegetation and scree, but there are interesting scrambles in the hollow below the back wall of crags, with a choice of easy escape routes onto the path climbing Birkett Edge.

Follow the ridge upwards to the apex of Dead Crags, with its excellent outlook over the upper Dash valley. The gently rounded Uldale fells in the background, the Skiddaw House road, the wooded gorge containing the cascades of Whitewater Dash, and the pastures around Dash Farm vividly portray the remote and largely untamed character of the landscape. Its character owes much to the relative failure of man's attempts to extend his control over the area. Although there is evidence of the enclosure of Dash Farm (which took place in 1660) in the fields surrounding the long, low seventeenth-century farmhouse on its slightly warmer south-west facing slope, the rushes and bracken in parts of the enclosed pastures clearly show the problems of drainage and field clearance on the fringe of permanent cultivation.

The higher fells have seen recent change of a different sort.

Most of the area of Skiddaw Forest was developed by the Lecon-field estate during the nineteenth century as a grouse moor, and it was only with the break-up of the estate in the 1950s that the careful management of the heather moor came to an end. Much of the heather has gone, displaced by bracken on the lower fells, bilberry on the higher slopes and grass almost anywhere. So the seemingly ageless landscape of Skiddaw Forest has seen a succession of vegetation, and has only recently assumed its present character. Thickly forested at one time, it is now virtu-ally treeless except for the occasional mountain ash in the deeper valleys and patches of juniper scrub; a heather moor as recently as the 1950s, it now presents a pattern of smooth-sided grassy fells interspersed with peat bog on the flatter summit ridges.

The top rocks of Dead Crags lie at about 2,100ft and only about two hundred yards north of the little-known summit of **Bakestall** (2,189ft), which is really no more than a slight pause in the downward sweep of Skiddaw's broad northern shoulder. But the summit, traversed by the boundary fence which has come up Birkett Edge, has a notable cairn and a fine view of the Scottish hills across the Solway Firth. The north ridge of Skiddaw forms the next stage of the route and has the advantage of being relatively easy and safe in poor visibility, since it is followed by the fence for much of the way. There is not much to divert the attention, however, on the way, and the extremely stony summit plateau of **Skiddaw** (3,053ft) will be greeted with some relief.

The fourth highest of the Lake District fells, Skiddaw (already visited in the Lakeland Horseshoe walk) often seems to have few friends and a host of detractors. The tedious ascent by the 'tourist route' is endlessly criticised, yet little is said about the excellent northern routes to the top, not only via Dead Crags and Bakestall, but also up Southerndale and along Ullock Pike and Longside Edge. Nevertheless, however the summit is gained, it has to be admitted that the highest ground holds no particular attractions. A rapid traverse of the long summit ridge, richly endowed with awkward slaty boulders, is called for and has the merit of an improving view all the way to **Skiddaw Little Man**

(2,837ft) which boasts as fine a panorama of the major fells in the Lake District as any other favourite viewpoint. The outlook from the summit cairn is all the more breathtaking because of the subtle interplay between lake and mountain, with Bowfell and the Scafell range especially prominent on the skyline behind Derwentwater, adorned with its wooded islands, and the north-western fells and their foothills framed behind Bassenthwaite Lake.

Regain the tourist path as it skirts the crest of Skiddaw Little Man, but leave it at the fence and follow this substantial boundary marker across the flat summit of Jenkin Hill. The fence (later a wall) heads directly for the summit of **Lonscale Fell** (2,344ft), which boasts only a small cairn in a flat and uneventful expanse of grass. The dull western approach to Lonscale Fell and the tedious area around the summit are soon forgotten, however, when the eastern rim of the summit plateau is visited. This is the feature which, when seen from the lower ground between Keswick and Threlkeld, gives the impression that Lonscale Fell has a small but graceful peak, steeply declining on all sides. It is an optical illusion, of course, but the sight of the eastern side of the fell, with its shattered cliffs plunging down to the Glenderaterra valley, provides a ready explanation for the error.

The more adventurous of two routes from Lonscale Fell to the Glenderaterra Beck descends directly from the eastern summit. This is an excellent scramble, with interest sustained by difficulties in route-finding, but it should only be attempted by the sure-footed (although Wainwright's stricture that 'this is not a route for descent' is a little over-protective). The initial view down the cliffs to the stream some 1,200ft below is intimidating, but this first section, a complex excrescence of shattered slate broken into miniature crags, separated by steep scree and precariously poised clumps of heather, can be skirted on steep grass to the left. In any case, it is nothing like as problematical as it first appears. Lower down there is still a good deal of scrambling, though the amount of exposed rock becomes rather less and there is time for a glance across the valley to the

western slopes of Blencathra. This is not the most attractive side
of that superb mountain, however, the projecting spur of Blease
Fell having more bulk than style.

At the foot of the north-east ridge, which eventually broadens
and becomes over-run with bracken, lies the track leading from
Skiddaw House to Keswick, which is some four miles away.
Turn left, towards Skiddaw House, and keep on the path above a
long-disused quarry to reach a junction of tracks at the foot of
the Burnt Horse ridge, close to a series of ruins (presumably
relics of past mining activity) and, even stranger, three walled
enclosures just above and to the west of the Glenderaterra Beck.

The Burnt Horse ridge is the key to the second and much less
strenuous descent from Lonscale Fell. Leave the summit in a
northerly direction, following the wall, and keep close to the
wall as far as the minor crags which occur about halfway down
the ridge. There is an excellent opportunity here to look across
and contemplate what might have been, for the rugged profile of
the north-east ridge commands the eye at this point. The Burnt
Horse ridge, rather tame in comparison, continues easily down
the ridge to join the Skiddaw House road about half a mile north
of the junction of tracks; ten minutes on this easy surface should
be enough to reach the junction.

Head down to the Glenderaterra, ford it, and take the path
rising to the right and crossing first Sinen Gill and then
Roughten Gill. Then keep to the main track as it contours
around Blease Fell. Down below, in the wide and marshy valley
bottom, are the remains of the former Roughten Gill mine, with
its associated levels and spoil heaps. Worked for lead in the nineteenth century, the mine was never particularly successful and
could not compete with the Newlands or Greenside ventures, or
even locally with the mines at Gategill and Woodend on the
southern slopes of Blencathra and closer to the main lines of
communication. The whole area is dotted with the disused
workings (which can be very dangerous and should not be
entered) of former mining enterprises, and there is another mine
shaft near the plantation lower down the valley.

The track skirting **Blease Fell**, superbly graded and generally fairly pleasant underfoot, continues southwards on its shelf above the Glenderaterra Beck, with excellent views across to Clough Head and the rocky north-western face of the Helvellyn range, in which Wanthwaite Crags and Bram Crag are especially prominent. Across the Glenderaterra valley, the roughly shaped eastern slopes of Lonscale Fell begin to assume their characteristic appearance; indeed, only Blease Fell is disappointing, with the magnificent scenery of Blencathra's southern face so near at hand but tantalisingly out of sight. Blease Fell offers little to quicken the pulse, with only an occasional abandoned quarry disturbing the rounded outline of the fell. Follow the track as it curves sharply left to pass the former Blencathra Sanatorium and the farm at High Row, and a little later a small disused quarry. The track has by now become a surfaced road, and it is feasible, if a little hard on the feet, to follow this into the village of **Threlkeld** (fully described in the relevant section of the Lakeland Horseshoe walk).

As usual there is a second possibility, avoiding roads at all costs. Fork left just past the quarry and take the field path which contours the hillside (the road dips sharply down at this point) and arrives at the farmyard at Blease. Continue eastwards, but on reaching the wooded valley of Blease Gill follow the stream down for a very pleasant half mile, with a delightfully attractive section just above the village. The stream and adjacent path reach the main road through Threlkeld (previously the A66 and very busy, but now much quieter since the village has been successfully bypassed) at a point fortuitously close to the two pubs.

3 BLENCATHRA
Threlkeld to Mungrisdale (8 miles/13km)

Any of the three central ridges, the four ravines or the two broad flanking fells which together make up the spectacular southern front of Blencathra can be used to reach the summit of this excellent mountain from Threlkeld. The most circuitous routes head for the flanks of the mountain, but Blease Fell and Scales

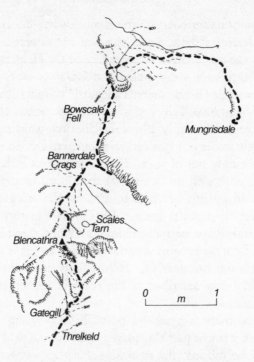

Bowscale
Fell

Mungrisdale

Bannerdale
Crags

Scales
Tarn

Blencathra

Gategill

Threlkeld

0   m   1

Fell are unexciting ways to conquer the dramatic south face. The ravines are undoubtedly better, but all deteriorate into frustratingly slow climbing over steep and rough ground in their upper parts, and naturally all are enclosed, with correspondingly restricted views. Of the three ridges, Doddick Fell is pleasant and surprisingly easy, but the most challenging are Gategill Fell, which includes a fine walk along a narrow ridge in its upper section (used for the descent from Blencathra by the Lakeland Horseshoe) and Hall's Fell.

There is some controversy over the true merit of the Hall's Fell ascent. Wainwright called it 'positively the finest way to any mountain-top in the district' (though whether he meant the Lake District as a whole or the district about which he was writing at the time, the northern fells, is not altogether clear). Harry Griffin has elected to disagree, although he acknowledges it as an excellent, airy route with magnificent views down into Doddick Gill and Gate Gill. Unquestionably, it is the connoisseur's way to the top of Blencathra, climbing steadily up through heather and then along a narrow and sometimes rather exposed knife-edge of rock directly to the summit of the mountain. There is no doubt that it is the best ascent in the northern fells, but in the Lake District as a whole there are other routes which are equally testing and just as spectacular.

Leave Threlkeld some way to the west of the church, at the junction of the main road through the village with the lane leading to the former sanatorium. The way is clearly marked along a grassy lane which leaves the junction to the right and is signposted 'Gategill and Blencathra via Hall's Fell'. Continue past a row of cottages and cut down slightly to the right of the lane to a footbridge crossing Blease Gill. Pass through the gate (again helpfully signposted to Hall's Fell) on the far side of the little wooded valley and gradually gain height diagonally across a series of fields. The path is clearly indicated at each field boundary by a prominent stile, and in any case it can be picked out on the ground as it heads towards a sturdy field barn. On reaching the barn, keep roughly to the same line across two more fields, pass through a five-barred gate and reach the cluster of buildings at **Gategill**. The farm and cottages give an impression of rural tranquillity now, but this was once an industrial hamlet, and the forlorn buildings of the disused mine still stand as a dilapidated memorial to those prosperous days. The Gategill mine, which reached its peak production in the late nineteenth century, was an important source of lead and zinc, and together with Wood-end and the other local mines provided employment for about a hundred men, transforming Threlkeld from a rural hamlet to a large, bustling industrial township.

Beyond the derelict mine buildings there is a junction of paths, at which the route lies uphill, to the left of a row of cottages and steeply up through the prettily wooded gorge of Gate Gill, with the beck tumbling alongside in an impressive series of cascades. The next minor landmark is a gate next to a well-built sheepfold, which can provide useful protection against driving rain. Ahead is the weir which regulated the flow of water to the mine, and higher up are yet more derelict buildings, one standing roofless in the sea of boulders brought down by the beck in spate. Towering above the scene is Hall's Fell, oppressively bulky at its base yet narrowing to lead straight to the summit of Blencathra (whose summit is also known as Hallsfell Top). The summit is just in view, poised above the steep fellside rising from the deep cleft of the Gate Gill ravine.

Cross the weir and zigzag up the path which is scored deeply into the fellside, so deeply that in places the surface cover of soil and vegetation has been completely worn away and the path rises awkwardly over exposed slabs of slaty rock. The initial stages are particularly steep, although there is some immediate consolation in the intimate views down into Gate Gill, a wild and stony gully sandwiched between stark rock buttresses. Eventually the path inclines away from the Gate Gill edge of the fell – there are just a couple of slightly tricky moments before it does so – and as the ridge narrows the path climbs through heather to a right-angled turn at about 1,500ft.

This sharp bend in the path occurs at a point where some comparatively level ground is reached after the hard slog from Gate Gill, and a rest on a comfortable couch of heather to review the scenery is almost irresistible. To the left is the serrated southern wall of Blencathra, with Doddick Fell and Scales Fell seen for the first time. Ahead is the valley of the River Glenderamackin, where the busy main road, lazy stream and silent track-bed of the former railway linking Keswick to the main line at Penrith snake successively across the picture. Beyond the wide valley can be seen the northern foothills of the Helvellyn range, rising to the first major summits of White Pike and Clough Head. The slopes are badly disfigured by the substantial gash of the Threlkeld roadstone quarry, a discordant and surprisingly large light-grey bowl in the middle of smooth greens and browns. Above the quarry, the site of the Iron Age settlement of Threlkeld Knotts can just about be picked out on a grassy shelf. To the right, the north-western fells form a tantalisingly alluring background beyond the jagged outline of Gategill Fell.

Sadly, it is necessary to turn away from this compelling scene to contemplate the harsh realities of the climb ahead. At first the

Narrow Edge, Blencathra

route lies steeply up through heather, keeping close now to the edge of the steep descent into the ravine containing Doddick Gill. Somehow this ravine seems a greener and less savage place than the forbidding gully of Gate Gill. As height is gained on the narrowing fellside, there is a sudden and dramatic view ahead of Narrow Edge and the top of Blencathra. The hard, but immensely rewarding, work begins here as the problems caused by the low crags, miniature towers and shattered slabs of Narrow Edge are faced and dealt with. Ruskin may have used this route in climbing Blencathra since he exultantly related that his ascent had included 'several bits of real crag work'.

At first the path keeps to the eastern side of the arête, just below the crest, and there are tremendous views straight down into Doddick Gill. Care is needed in one or two places, and this is not a place to stop and contemplate at leisure when a fresh westerly wind is blowing. Later, the simplest route lies just to the west of the edge, and higher up the western side is much to be preferred, with the gentler slope down towards Gate Gill causing fewer palpitations than the precipitous descent to Doddick Gill. For much of the route the way lies over easy rock slabs, with occasional scrambles on generous holds in the shattered slates up minor crags and through little rock gateways. Narrow Edge comes to an end just below the summit, and there is an easy scramble on loose worn rock up to the cairn marking the top of **Blencathra** (2,847ft), which is superbly poised on the very edge of the summit plateau.

Keep to the right across the unexpectedly large and level plateau, which dips slightly below Hallsfell Top and the upper rim of Foule Crag to the north. The dip gives rise to Blencathra's alternative and more prosaic name of Saddleback, which is much less awe-inspiring than Blencathra, meaning 'the hill of the devils'. This right-hand edge of the saddle enjoys an extraordinary prospect eastwards into the deep, dark bowl containing Scales Tarn, with the arête of Sharp Edge poised above and beyond the tarn. The grassy plateau itself can claim only a small and seasonal tarn, which pales into insignificance compared with **Scales Tarn**, imprisoned behind a glacial moraine in a hollow scooped out by ice a thousand feet below the top of Tarn Crags, its solidly built and almost perpendicular back wall. In fact the tarn is remarkably shallow, a mere 26ft deep at most, although early writers, perhaps understandably awestruck by its situation in the shadow of huge crags rising steeply to the top of Blencathra, regarded it as bottomless.

To the north Scales Tarn is hemmed in by the delicate arête of Sharp Edge, its crest offering a challenging walk almost entirely on rock. This walk is a good deal easier than it appears from above; the path to the edge can be seen dropping steeply down from Blencathra's summit tableland close to the brooding wall of Foule Crag. Keep above the rim of the crag, detouring left if desired to the white memorial cross laid out in the grass or to search for the stone stripes and stone polygons formed by frost action. Next, descend the steep stony slope which, for obvious reasons, is known as Blue Screes. This slope leads to the col at the head of the long and twisting valley of the River Glenderamackin (which, it will be recalled, has already been seen in the village of Mungrisdale right at the start of the Back o' Skidda' walk and also, remarkably enough, on the other side of

Blencathra). A superbly constructed green track goes down on the left-hand side of the valley, skirts Bannerdale Crags and leads into Mungrisdale, and this path can be used if the weather is deteriorating.

Look back from the col to the profile of Foule Crag and Sharp Edge, and then press on eastwards over hummocky grass to the summit ridge of **Bannerdale Crags** (2,230ft). The mile-long escarpment of Bannerdale Crags, formed of Skiddaw Slates hardened by metamorphism, is a dominating feature of the Glenderamackin valley, but from above (and especially when seen immediately after the extraordinary rock architecture which is the hallmark of Blencathra) it appears to be of no real consequence. There is a small cairn composed of angular slaty boulders at the summit, set slightly away from the top of the crags, and at the base of the crag are the scanty remains of a lead mine, with old levels, fairly substantial caves and a derelict mine building.

A mile or so to the north of Bannerdale Crags is the final summit to be attained, that of Bowscale Fell. The intervening ground can be covered fairly quickly, although it is advisable to bear well to the right, along the edge of the crags, where the view is better and the ground firmer. At the col, the path from Mungrisdale to the upper Caldew valley and Skiddaw House, its route on the boggy ground at the crest of the ridge marked by a few upright stone slabs, is crossed, and the shoulder of **Bowscale Fell** (2,306ft) is climbed very easily to a wind-shelter which has seen better days but which also serves as a summit cairn. There is very little else in the area of the summit, although the 2½in map indicates a rash of bench marks sited, for some obscure but no doubt worthy reason, both here and lower down on the slopes near Long Gill.

It would be easy, on the evidence so far, to dismiss Bowscale Fell as rounded, grassy and deadly dull, but this would be completely wrong. A short walk north reveals the one priceless asset of the fell: the solid cliff of Tarn Crag with, nestling at its foot, Bowscale Tarn. This corrie tarn is the furthest north in the Lake District, but without doubt it is among the very best. A dark, north-facing tarn trapped by an extensive glacial moraine,

Bowscale Tarn was a firm favourite with the Victorians, particularly after two myths became widespread. First, it was claimed that the pool was so deep and so dark that even on a fine summer's day the stars could be seen reflected in its waters – pure nonsense, of course, but very good box-office. Secondly, the tarn became famous as the home of two immortal fish, a story which even moved Wordsworth to verse (but then, a host of things in the Lakes had that effect). Times change, and the once-popular path from the hamlet of Bowscale to its tarn is now suffering badly from neglect, having become overgrown in places and marshy where it meets streams coursing down the fellside.

Two routes are feasible from the top of Tarn Crags. A left turn leads eventually to a tongue of grass between rocky buttresses which can be used to get down to the tarn and join the path used by the Victorians. The path, well above the Caldew valley, eventually leads above a series of small fields into the hamlet of Bowscale, with Mungrisdale only about half a mile or so away by road. A right turn above Tarn Crags leads along the undulating east ridge of Bowscale Fell, with good views of the tarn in its craggy hollow, and then heads down through the heather to the top of Raven Crags, which can be negotiated safely on a path meandering down to an unsurfaced lane on the outskirts of **Mungrisdale**. Where the lane meets the surfaced road, turn right (the road sign announcing the village is in view) and follow the road round a sharp bend, with the unusual post office off to the right, to reach Mungrisdale Church.

It is well worth while continuing along the road, around two more sharp bends, to explore the rest of this delightful village. After the second bend, a roughly surfaced lane leads off to the right (there is a telephone box on the corner); walk along this to the fell gate and continue along the track for a few hundred yards. After crossing a subsidiary stream the route forks: the left branch is the track which follows the Glenderamackin to the col below Foule Crag on Blencathra, while the right fork leads into Bannerdale, where the long line of crags can be seen at the valley head.

Back on the road through Mungrisdale, take the next road

right (after only 20 yards) across the high bridge spanning the little gorge of the Glenderamackin, which at this point rushes over large, flat, slaty slabs, and seek out The Mill Inn, a genuinely unspoilt village inn which has recently begun to serve real ale. This road leads past the pub around Souther Fell to Scales and Threlkeld, and makes an interesting and relaxing stroll. The main road can be seen on the other side of the river (there is a footbridge by The Mill Inn) and this leads, in about two miles, to the Keswick–Penrith road and public transport.

THE ROMAN WAY

This is a five-day walk which is full of interest to the historian, yet also contrives to offer a great deal more besides. It traces the route chosen by the Romans to impress their authority on the Lake District, visiting the remains of the four Roman forts of Brocavum, Galava, Mediobogdum and Glannaventa, and also the rich archaeological remains of the Moor Divock area. At the same time it tackles one of the finest and longest Lakeland ridge walks, the High Street range, crosses the infamous Wrynose and Hardknott passes using alternatives to the narrow, tortuous and congested roads which thread their way across, and finishes with a tranquil journey down the unspoilt and picturesque valley of Eskdale to the sea at Ravenglass.

1 NORTH-EASTERN FOOTHILLS
Brougham to Howtown (12 miles/19km)

The route starts at the grass-covered remains of the Roman fort of **Brocavum**, in the Eamont valley just south-east of the outskirts of Penrith. The Roman remains are frankly disappointing; not so the adjacent Brougham Castle, which dates from the thirteenth century. The Roman fort, built in the second century AD and occupied for a couple of hundred years, commanded the ford crossing the Eamont and attracted quite a sizeable civilian settlement on the banks of the river. Brougham Castle partially obscures the remains of the fort, but the low banks of the enclosing walls are still visible to the south-east of the castle.

The oldest surviving feature of Brougham Castle is the massive but rather decayed keep, dating from about 1203. Much of the

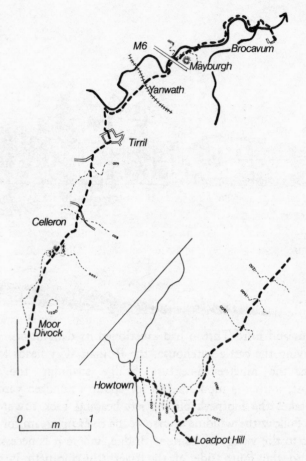

remainder is late thirteenth or early fourteenth century, a period when considerable rebuilding took place. This included the reconstruction of the keep to accommodate a passage to an inner gatehouse, a highly unusual feature. The two gatehouses, the chapel and the south-west tower (which commands an extremely wide distant prospect of the Lakeland hills, with Blencathra prominent) all date from this period. Later, the castle was raided by the Scots and fell into disrepair before Lady Anne Clifford began a thorough restoration in 1651–2. The foundations of the bakehouse and brewhouse in the courtyard date from Lady Anne's time. By 1700, however, the castle was once again

Brougham Castle

ruinous and Lord Tufton had sanctioned its demolition.

Leaving the castle gatehouse, the Roman Way heads for and crosses the nineteenth-century bridge spanning the River Eamont, joins the modern A66 for about a hundred yards and then takes the footpath on the left heading back towards the river. Follow the winding course of the river upstream for about a mile to the village of Eamont Bridge, where it is necessary to cross to the south side of the river (the footpath is clearly signposted to Yanwath). The present bridge dates from the sixteenth century, but this has always been an important crossing point. Until the thirteenth century the river acted from time to time as the border with Scotland, and until 1974 it formed the boundary between Cumberland and Westmorland. Eamont Bridge contains a number of attractive old houses, including the Mansion House, studied seventeenth-century Baroque. At the south end of the village are the rather feeble remains of King Arthur's Round Table, a circular double-entrance henge monument badly damaged by road construction.

The footpath to Yanwath turns away from the river about

two hundred yards upstream from Eamont Bridge and skirts the northern boundary of the far more impressive henge monument at **Mayburgh**. Here there are substantial earthworks; the encircling bank, some two hundred feet across, still reaches a height of up to fifteen feet, and the rounded boulders used in its construction have been exposed in places. There is a single eastern entrance, and one standing stone is still there, in the centre of the circle. Eighteenth-century accounts talk of four such stones inside the circle and two pairs of standing stones at the entrance. The purpose of these henge monuments, thought to have been constructed in the late Neolithic or early Bronze Age, is not at all clear, although about seventy have been discovered in Britain.

The path continues past Mayburgh, turns right and then left to pass under the M6 motorway, rejoins the Eamont for a while and then heads slightly south of west to the hamlet of **Yanwath**, passing under the main line railway. Away to the right can be seen the impressive pele tower which is the oldest part of Yanwath Hall. The pele was erected in 1323 by John de Sutton, and the rest of the attractive building, consisting of hall, kitchen and courtyard, was added in the fifteenth century. The pele is an excellent example of its type, with a massive tunnel-vaulted ground floor, mullioned and transomed first-floor windows and stark sandstone battlements.

Head across a series of fields from Yanwath, keeping close company yet again with the Eamont, and then, just downstream from a footbridge across the river, swing sharply to the left, now travelling south across rising ground to the cluster of houses at Sockbridge, where the hall consists of two ranges placed at right angles to one another. The road from Penrith to Pooley Bridge is soon encountered. Just to the left is the large but quite attractive village of **Tirril**; its older buildings front onto a triangular green, but it has a lot of recent housing, presumably aimed at Penrith commuters or the affluent retired. The Queen's Head, formerly supplied by the village's own brewery (Siddle's, who ceased brewing in 1907), still sells an excellent pint of bitter and is handily placed for a lunch-time snack.

The route of High Street, the Roman road, can be traced south-west from Tirril, but there is no continuous right of way and so a short detour along the B5320 is inevitable. After a quarter of a mile turn left, taking a lane which climbs steadily to the farm at **Celleron**. Keep straight ahead, then bear right to pass Winder Hall and, with the course of the Roman road now underfoot, skirt the limestone summit of Heughscar Hill, a mere 1,231ft high yet with wide views to the Scottish hills and across to the Pennines. The Roman road here is a green track undulating pleasantly through the bracken, with a fine outlook to the right over the lower reaches of Ullswater and across to the rounded northern representatives of the Helvellyn range.

On the southern flanks of Heughscar Hill the broad track from Pooley Bridge to Heltonhead is crossed, and the way lies south along a deeply rutted and often swampy path to The Cockpit, variously described as an unobtrusive stone circle, a large ring cairn and an ancient upland hamlet whose circular wall protected a handful of huts. With a diameter of 120ft, the Cockpit can boast some sixty-five stones but only one of them is still upright and many of the rest have subsided in a rather undignified way into the grass and bracken.

This area of **Moor Divock** was an important centre in the Bronze Age, and archaeologists have identified the sites of no less than seven stone circles on these fells. Even to the layman the prehistoric remains littering this wild moor are strangely evocative. To the east of the Cockpit is an unusual and quite impressive cairn circle, and a quarter of a mile further on towards Heltonhead is the Cop Stone, a broad and isolated 5ft monolith which, sadly, is not really worth the detour from the Roman road. It once formed part of yet another stone circle, and it is just possible to make out traces of the bank inside which the other stones stood. The moor is pockmarked with tumuli, many of them overgrown with bracken and hard to discern, and there are other unexplained mounds and hollows.

At the Cockpit the Roman Way alters course to the south-west and begins to ascend the northern bastions of the High Street range. The line of the path is not always clear underfoot at

first as it rises wetly out of the gathering grounds of the Elder
Beck and away from Moor Divock. Nevertheless, the general
south-westerly direction is maintained across the slopes of Barton
Fell, keeping well to the left of White Knott and, later on,
Arthur's Pike and Bonscale Pike, both of which present steep and
rocky faces to Ullswater but can only lay claim to gentle grassy
slopes barren of interest on their eastern flanks. The path, by
now well marked, gains height very gradually indeed, passing a
motley collection of covered reservoirs and occasional boundary
stones. South of Arthur's Pike the easy slopes to the right are
suddenly interrupted by the deeply inset valley of Swarthbeck
Gill, with Bonscale Pike beyond. On the far side of the summit
stands Bonscale Tower, together with a second and less attractive
beacon some distance to the south; these are the bold features
which so clearly identify the summit from across Ullswater.

The Roman Way ignores Bonscale Pike (the conquest of
which would involve only a short detour but a good deal of extra
climbing) and continues towards Loadpot Hill, passing the
Standing Stone, a forlorn relic of yet another stone circle, above
the head of Swarthbeck Gill, and then passing the gloomy
hollow of Loadpot Hole. The Roman road swings right to avoid
the highest ground on Loadpot Hill. On these northern slopes of
the hill a section of the road was excavated to reveal a foundation
of quarried boulders 2ft thick below 8in of peat, a similar depth
of gravel and a surface cover of turf. Now there are few indications of the antiquity of the route, but it is still a broad, fast
walkers' highway.

The summit of **Loadpot Hill** (2,201ft) is marked only by an
uninteresting expanse of grass, and it is easy to see why the
Romans chose to avoid it. The cairn, a modest pile of quartz
boulders surrounding a boundary stone, decorates an almost
arbitrary spot in the extensive sheepwalk. What used to distin-
guish the scene and set Loadpot Hill apart from other Lakeland
fells lay two or three hundred yards south of the cairn, and the
substantial remains are still to be seen. This was Lowther House,
a shooting lodge belonging to the Lowther estate, and it was
dramatically sited in an exposed location north of the col

between Loadpot Hill and its equally bulky and rounded southern neighbour, Wether Hill. When its original use ceased, the majority of the structure was demolished, but the stone fireplace and gaunt, towering chimney stack lived on as an unmistakable landmark and a welcome oasis of colour in these rather uneventful uplands. Sadly, the frost, rains and gales of Lakeland winters wrought havoc on the unprotected structure, and it was progressively reduced in height until, in 1973, the final collapse took place. Now the rubble lies scattered around the fellside, a rare outbreak of stones in the encircling wastes of heather and peat bog.

Ideally, the walk should now continue across Wether Hill to the greater excitement further south along the High Street range, finally dropping down into the Trout Beck valley after traversing the ridge from the foothills at Tirril to its climax on High Street itself and Thornthwaite Crag. But for most walkers, who will understandably have taken some time to reach Tirril from Brougham, this is too arduous an expedition to be contemplated for a single day. The only real alternative is to descend to Howtown, where a limited amount of accommodation is available, and then to regain the ridge at Loadpot Hill on the following day. Some variation of routes is possible in order to avoid too strong a feeling of déjà vu on the way back up from Howtown.

In descent, the simplest method is to track over from the summit of Loadpot Hill to the line of the Roman road on its western flank, head north and then leave the road to the left where it alters course sharply. Pass a couple of small and shallow tarns and keep well above the broken rocks and steep scree of Brock Crag. There is an increasingly delightful prospect ahead of Ullswater, framed in its setting of low hills, and to the left can be seen the quiet valleys of Martindale. Beyond Brock Crag follow the graded path down to the intake wall above the farmhouse at Mellguards. Below the fell gate a track leads down to Fusedale Beck and the rough lane heading down the valley to the hotel in the little hamlet of **Howtown**. There is really no more than the hotel and a cluster of cottages, yet the hamlet is well known for two reasons: it is served by the steamer service on Ullswater and lies at the northern end of the justifiably famous low-level walk from Patterdale via Silver Point.

It is well worth strolling along the narrow lane leading from Howtown into the unfrequented valleys on the eastern side of Ullswater. Some distance away from Howtown is the late nineteenth-century church of St Peter, an extravagant piece of urban Victoriana which looks distinctly out of place in the Lake District. A further half mile up the valley of the Howegrain Beck is the much more attractive dale chapel of St Martin, a simple structure with nave and chancel all in one. There was a church here in the fourteenth century, but it was completely reconstructed in 1633. Finally, beyond the older church the dale splits into the two tributary valleys of Bannerdale and the Rampsgill Beck, divided by The Nab, the fell which lies at the heart of the ancient Martindale deer forest; but walkers are unwelcome here, and there is little choice but to return to Howtown.

2 HIGH STREET
Howtown to Troutbeck (13 miles/21km)

The first target on this comparatively tough day's walk is the summit plateau of **Loadpot Hill**, the object which has dominated proceedings since the wet expanse of Moor Divock was negotiated. Purists may insist on retracing their steps back up past Mellguards and Brock Crag to the summit cairn; others will continue along the pleasant valley of Fusedale and, after crossing Dodd Gill, take the path rising through bracken on its south bank and then, above the headwaters of the gill, bear directly east to reach the Roman road as it negotiates the flat sheepwalk comprising the summit area of Loadpot Hill. Turn right and follow the Roman road past the remains of the Lowther House chimney down to the col separating the Fusedale Beck to the right from the unknown valley of Cawdale Beck to the left.

The area down on the left, containing the sources of the many

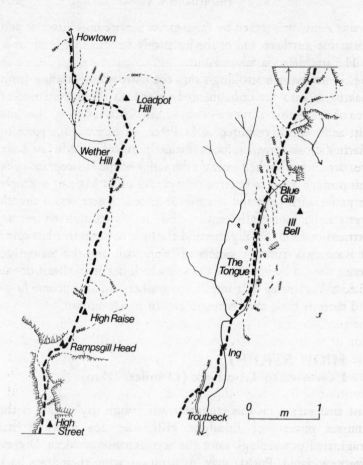

small streams which feed the Cawdale Beck, is evocatively named on the maps as the White Bog, and for a short distance the going on the ridge is equally sticky. A series of deep peat groughs faintly reminiscent of those in the Peak District has to be negotiated before the ground begins to rise easily to the northern summit of **Wether Hill** (2,210ft). The southerly summit is more extensive but is in fact slightly lower, and its northerly twin celebrates this fact with a small cairn supporting a wooden stake; there is nothing else of interest here, although the view is extensive and includes much of the Pennines away to the left and, across the Martindale deer forest, Helvellyn and Fairfield. There

is also a hint in the far distance of the Scafell range and, somewhat unexpectedly, the Old Man of Coniston.

The route is perfectly obvious along the narrowing ridge, with
the combination of easy gradients and wiry, close-cropped grass
making for fast walking at least as far as the next col, another
area of peat trenches where Keasand Sike falls away steeply to the
left, and then, in company with a wall which has come up from
Martindale, past the subsidiary height of Red Crag and the reedy
area around Redcrag Tarn. The track continues, very plainly at
this point, on the west side of the wall (though the east side may
be preferred if high winds are sweeping across from the south-
west) and climbs the shoulder of Raven Howe, then skirts an
extraordinary and savagely eroded ravine containing a tributary
of Rampsgill Beck (the wall parts company here, following the
ravine down) and studiously ignores the summit of **High Raise**
(2,634ft).

The summit is worth the minor detour, however, since it is
the second highest in the High Street range. Perhaps in recognition of this superior altitude, there is an area of boulders around
the summit cairn which is itself much larger than those on the
lower fells away to the north-east. A rough wind-shelter
constructed from the indigenous stones lies a little to the south-
east and adds further to the impression that High Raise is the
first real mountain to be traversed on the walk. There are fine
crags, too, but these (Whelter Crags) are a mile away to the east,
overlooking Haweswater.

Regain the Roman road and continue round above the vast
bowl containing Rampsgill Beck, with the line of shattered crags
at the valley head becoming increasingly impressive on the way
down to a shallow depression. Keep close to the edge of the
broken line of crags and then climb gently to the top of
Rampsgill Head (2,581ft), marked by a rather tumbledown
cairn. A more notable cairn slightly further north indicates the
top of the crags, and the stroll across to it should not be missed,
for the rock architecture is good by any standards and outstanding in the context of the High Street range. The more northerly
cairn also has a tremendous bird's-eye view of Rampsgill, with

Ullswater beyond, and the Fairfield and Helvellyn ranges well to the fore on the western horizon.

From Rampsgill Head the route continues south-west above Twopenny Crag to the Straits of Riggindale, where the good path from Patterdale (which forms part of the Lakeland Horseshoe) joins from the right and the ridge narrows dramatically. Hayeswater, now a reservoir for Penrith, lies down on the right, and to the left is a magnificent vista along the glacial trough of Riggindale to the much larger reservoir of Haweswater. The far wall of Riggindale has been eroded back to help form the arête of Long Stile, below which lies Caspel Gate with its diminutive tarn.

Although the ridge is at its narrowest at this point, there is still a choice of three routes south towards the summit of High Street. A fair path follows the eastern rim, above Riggindale and Long Stile, in order to capture the finest views (see the Lakeland Horseshoe for details). The middle course keeps to the substantial boundary wall which heads more or less straight for the summit, and can act as a useful shelter against wind and rain. The Roman road inclines towards the western edge of the ridge, although not with the daring indicated on some OS maps, for the crags shown are more minor and rather further away from the track than would appear to be the case.

The rutted track following the line of the Roman road is all too visible as it rises gradually across the grassy plateau, although it needs a fertile imagination to deduce any link between the present path and the road engineered through the peat by the Romans. The sodden layer of peat which had displaced the primeval forest on the ridge (though not in the valleys) will have caused problems in places during the construction of the road, and the patches of marsh and peat hags which still have to be negotiated offer silent testimony to the scale of the Romans' achievement. The unrelenting flatness of the broad ridge is the real problem, and it has the secondary effect of robbing the ascent of much of its interest. Progress seems painfully slow and there is little sense of achievement.

Eventually the triangulation column marking the top of **High**

Street (2,718ft) comes into view in its gap in the wall running the length of the summit plateau. The summit is set well back from the best scenery which the mountain has to offer, and it is worth walking across the wiry, coarse grass to the eastern edge of the plateau, which has marvellous views down to Blea Water, the third deepest sheet of water in the Lake District and almost encircled by crags, and along Long Stile and Rough Crag to the bleached shores of Haweswater. The summit plateau itself was the scene of an annual shepherds' meet and fair day until 1835.

South of the Ordnance Survey pillar the wall continues its journey along the crest of the ridge and the line of the Roman road, which lies well to its west at first, gradually converges with the wall, then continues straight ahead when the wall dives down the fellside towards the upper reaches of Hayeswater Gill. To the right lies Thornthwaite Crag, its 14ft beacon tower a reassuringly certain landmark in mist. On the other side of the ridge is the upper Kentmere valley, a little-known but particularly attractive dalehead hemmed in by Froswick and Ill Bell to the west and Mardale Ill Bell and Harter Fell to the north and east. The small reservoir enhances the scene and the gaunt mass of Rainsborrow Crag completes a memorable picture.

The route of the Roman road allows a leisurely contemplation of this scene as it continues south along the ridge, with Froswick looming ahead, but instead of beginning the ascent of this fell the route bears right and heads down towards the Troutbeck valley. It is easy to be seduced by the excellent scenery of upper Kentmere and the welcoming slopes of Froswick into following the ridge path too far south, but this is a mistake to be avoided at all costs, since it is difficult to pick up the Roman Way again. A diagonal route to join it in the valley bottom is ruled out by the deep and extremely rough trench of **Blue Gill**, and a direct descent of the fellside can easily become a desperate scramble on steep, slippery grass and loose boulders.

The Roman road itself follows a comparatively steep course as it leaves the ridge and slants down Scot Rake, so called because border raiders used the existing route from the north in their incursions during the Middle Ages. The rake, a green track in

*Yoke, Ill Bell and Froswick
from the Troutbeck Valley*

the bracken, descends quickly to a gate in a particularly solid wall at the bottom of the valley; Blue Gill here is a sparkling, clear stream and a useful source of moisture towards the end of a hot day.

Follow the path across a level and often rather damp sheep pasture, and then keep to the improving track as it follows Hagg Gill downstream. The track passes close to a couple of rather undistinguished burial mounds and then, on the far side of the stream, a substantial and cavernous quarry which has led to the fellside here – part of the lower reaches of **Ill Bell**, though without the rugged character of the summit or the Kentmere side of the mountain – becoming known as Quarry Brow. The quarry is approached by a track which used to ford the stream and which can still be seen leaving the main route along the valley at an acute angle and down a steep gradient which must have tested the quarry wagons.

A little lower down the valley there is a second and equally substantial quarry, called Park Quarry after the important sheep farm of Troutbeck Park which lies just round the corner. The quarry track can be used to cross the stream and join the fair path leading down the east bank, but the western path leads more directly to Troutbeck. Hagg Gill, which has previously been pursuing an open and rather nondescript course, here enters a highly attractive little ravine, with mountain ash in abundance and some precipitous rock outcrops. The excellent path now proceeds amidst subdued scenery, losing height slowly, between the bulky and rather tame flanks of Yoke and the slopes of Troutbeck Tongue. Once more it is noticeable how so many Lakeland fells confine their grandeur to one side, and certainly Yoke follows this pattern, for there is no hint on this rather dreary western face of the splendidly plunging precipice of Rainsborrow Crag just beyond the summit ridge.

The view back up the valley is certainly not dreary, and this is the time to savour it because the path downstream now diverges slightly from Hagg Gill and rounds the lower slopes of **The Tongue**. The line of the Roman road can be traced all the way back up the valley to Thornthwaite Crag, its beacon being just discernible on the skyline, and to the right is the solid line of fells making up the Ill Bell ridge. The track leads down towards Troutbeck Park, the farm once owned by Beatrix Potter; she lived at Hill Top Farm in Near Sawrey, on the other side of Windermere, but bought Troutbeck Park to preserve its character as a former medieval deer park turned statesman farm. Beatrix Potter bequeathed the farm to the National Trust, but it is not open to the public and the route turns away from it by taking the signposted footpath to the left and crossing a field, where the path is ill defined but the general direction obvious.

The path rejoins the track at the far side of the field, and then keeps to the flat valley floor of the Trout Beck, divided into its patchwork of irregularly shaped little fields, to **Ing Bridge**, a good viewpoint for the flood defence work carried out in an attempt to tame the viciously swirling torrent into which this quiet stream is periodically transformed in winter. Further downstream, the less acceptable works of man, here catering for caravans and tents, intrude into the scene below the long line of the Garburn road, the once-important packhorse track from

Troutbeck to Kentmere, etched into the hillside as it slowly climbs out of the Trout Beck valley.

Half a mile downstream from Ing Bridge there is a choice of routes. Straight on lies a very pleasant footpath which leads through trees to the main road (A592), where the lane opposite heads for the centre of the straggling collection of statesman farms which makes up the village of **Troutbeck**. The track inclining uphill to the right leads directly to the cluster of dwellings at Town Head, and perhaps a much-needed pint of real ale in The Queen's Head, after which the quiet lane forming the main street of Troutbeck can be followed southwards to explore the attractions of the village (see the Lakeland Horseshoe for details). It is more than a mile, however, to the National Trust's showpiece farmhouse at Town End, which may deter some who have just completed the long haul over High Street from Howtown.

3   THE BRATHAY VALLEY
Troutbeck to Little Langdale (9 miles/14km)

After the exertions involved in the previous day's walk over the High Street range, this is an easy low-level walk, with the modest height of Wansfell Pike the only peak to be attained, but there is plenty to see in the town of Ambleside, the Roman fort of Galava and along the banks of the River Brathay, with the two waterfalls of Skelwith Force and Colwith Force the high-

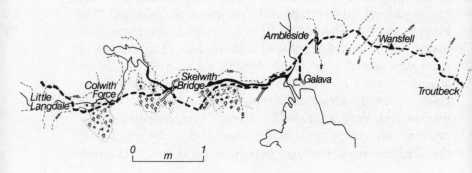

lights of the day. The exact line of the Roman road is uncertain throughout most of the walk, though it must have coincided in places with the present road into Little Langdale. This narrow road can be appallingly busy in summer, and so the route seeks out quiet paths and lanes closer to the river.

The Roman road probably traversed the southern slopes of Wansfell to reach the fort of Galava on the shores of Windermere, but a more appealing prospect for the present-day walker is to reach Ambleside across the top of Wansfell Pike and so take in the magnificent view of Windermere from this craggy southern extremity of the otherwise unexceptional Wansfell ridge. Take the track, signposted to Ambleside, heading westwards some eighty yards north of St Margaret's Well in the village of **Troutbeck**. This track, known as Nanny Lane, can be muddy after rain where it leads crookedly up, steeply at first, through the trees onto the open fellside. After half a mile or so a footpath leads over a stile to the left and this path, which is amply waymarked with cairns and wooden posts, heads directly for **Wansfell Pike** (1,581ft).

The journey so far has been uneventful but in the last few strides to the ridge top it changes character completely as a tremendous view unfolds to the south and west. The eye will be taken immediately by the almost unparalleled prospect along the gently curving length of Windermere in its shallow and well-wooded valley. Round to the right is the finely grouped ridge of the Coniston Fells, from the Old Man to Wetherlam, and further right is the Scafell range and Great Gable behind Crinkle Crags, Bowfell and the Langdale Pikes.

Below Wansfell Pike lies the typically Lakeland slate town of Ambleside, which is reached by a straightforward, though at times quite steep, path descending by the side of a tributary of the Stock Ghyll (this is one of the few cases where the picturesque Victorian affectation of 'ghyll' rather than 'gill' has become so entrenched that it has to be accepted). After crossing Blue Hill Road and the lane to Middle Grove, turn left and follow the path down the main valley to Stockghyll Force, one of the earliest and most visited of the Victorians' discoveries, but still highly attractive after prolonged rainfall as it crashes over a rock step and through a tightly constricted gorge overgrown with trees, ferns and mosses. The total height of the falls is about seventy feet.

The original focus of settlement at **Ambleside** was in the area known as Above Stock, high above the little gorge of Stock Ghyll. This is still the most pleasant part of town to visit, with its ancient grey farmhouses, diminutive chapel and superb traditional pub, The Golden Rule, on Smithy Brow. The first settlers chose this spot partly because it was well above the marshy Rothay flood plain and partly because they harnessed the fast-flowing Stock Ghyll to provide the power for at least half a dozen mills – corn mills, fulling mills, a bobbin mill, bark mills and a paper mill. The former corn mill on the north bank of Stock Ghyll has been restored fairly recently, and the overshot wheel with a diameter of 16ft, which could be thought to be antique, is in fact a reproduction dating from 1973. The mill dates from the fourteenth century, and by 1639 was in the hands of the Braithwaite family. Corn was ground here until the early years of the twentieth century, but the Old Mill is now a pottery and shop. Further upstream, a former bobbin mill has been converted into holiday flats.

The old slate-grey cottages around Chapel Hill in Above Stock are solidly built of the local stone and are characterised by thick walls and small windows. The most revealing of the buildings in this part of Ambleside is How Head. Some of the stone used to build it has been shown to have come from the fort at Galava, and part of the interior is still in its original condition with features dating from the sixteenth century. Around the corner is St Anne's Hall, the former church but now a parish hall. The first chapel on this site was built in the second half of the fifteenth century (previously Ambleside was merely part of Grasmere parish) but the present rather plain building dates from 1812. Ambleside's nineteenth-century growth was so rapid, however, that by 1852 a larger church was required. This was designed by Sir George Gilbert Scott and built on lower ground near the newer housing, and gradually St Anne's chapel became redundant.

Ambleside's first market charter was granted to the Countess of Pembroke in 1650, and indeed the centre of the town is still the market place, though it is now crowded with gift shops and tourists rather than sheep. The decline of the market (it lapsed in about 1825 and has only recently been revived) could have led to the virtual death of Ambleside but the boom in tourism arrived at just the right time, and it now utterly dominates the town. Its worst effects can be seen in the Bridge House, the infamous tiny eighteenth-century summerhouse straddling Stock Ghyll, which now serves as an information centre for the National Trust; in the exaggerated prominence given to the annual rushbearing ceremony in July; and in the appalling traffic problems which beset the town in summer.

Unfortunately, there is little respite from the traffic during the half-mile trek to Borrans Field, the site of **Galava** Roman fort, although a footpath does cut off one section of the main road. The first fort on this site was constructed of timber with turf ramparts in the first century AD on the alluvial flats at the head of Windermere, and close to the confluence of the Brathay and Rothay. Not surprisingly it was subject to flooding, and during Hadrian's reign (about 122 AD) it was replaced by a stone-built fort on slightly higher ground, which was occupied until the fourth century. Traces of the foundations of the walls and major buildings can be discerned, but this is the least impressive of the Roman forts in the Lake District, and a visit to the National Park Centre at Brockhole, two miles south on the shores of Windermere, is recommended to see the excavated remains and an interesting reconstruction of the later fort.

Return to the bridge over the River Rothay, which is here nearing the end of its journey from Steel Fell above Grasmere, and take the road westwards to Clappersgate. This is the main road from Ambleside to Coniston, but for half a mile there is no real alternative except for the wide grassy verge. At Clappersgate – at one time the immediate destination for slate from Great Langdale which was loaded onto barges and sent down Windermere – is the White Craggs rock garden, a collection of alpine and rock plants among the craggy lower slopes of Loughrigg

Fell. Clappersgate now consists of a few cottages, many of them dating from the seventeenth century, huddled at the base of the fell.

Immediately on the left across the bridge (whose central arch collapsed in 1681) is Old Brathay, built in the 1790s and sold in 1799 to Charles Lloyd, a prominent Birmingham banker. The farm here also served as a public house in the eighteenth century. Slightly further south is The Croft, formerly a hotel with an excellent position at the head of the lake but now converted into luxury flats.

The Roman Way crosses the bridge over the Brathay, then takes the lane leaving the Hawkshead road on the right after a hundred yards or so, and keeps close to the river bank as far as Clappersgate Church, an incongruous Italianate building dating from 1836. The quiet lane to Skelwith Fold is then taken through well-wooded and gentle countryside. Turn right at Skelwith Fold, keep right at a junction of lanes and head down past the school house to rejoin the river at **Skelwith Bridge**.

Take the good footpath signposted south of the bridge and follow the Brathay upstream to Skelwith Force, much visited because of its accessibility from the road but actually no more than a series of rapids, with foaming cascades but an overall fall of only about fifteen feet. Nevertheless the Brathay is a sizeable river at this point, and the effect of a considerable volume of water crashing into the narrow rocky channel after a few days of Lakeland rain is dramatic. Return to the road and turn right, then take the signposted footpath travelling west past Park House to Elterwater Park and Low Park. The names indicate that these farms were outlying sheep farms of Furness Abbey, probably coming into existence in the fourteenth or fifteenth century. To the north is an excellent view of the junction of the rivers draining the two Langdales in the reedy lake of Elterwater.

Cross a minor road and take the well-made path to **Colwith Force**, the second of the Brathay's waterfalls and infinitely the more impressive. This is where the side valley of Little Langdale, effectively a 'hanging' valley, joins Great Langdale, with its stream tumbling down a 50ft rock step to reach the more heavily

Slater Bridge Little Langdale

glaciated main valley floor. Once a noted tourist attraction, Colwith Force fell from favour and the approach to it became overgrown and neglected, but remedial work carried out by the National Trust has much improved the position, and the cascading water in its woodland setting can once more be appreciated.

The route now follows a path which cuts across the wood from Colwith Force to High Park, another of the sheep farms which Furness Abbey created from the fells, and then takes the farm lane running between High Park and Stang End. Across the valley is Hacket, a farm whose name crops up twice in historical documents. In the early sixteenth century it was listed as one of a number of farms which had been created by illegal enclosure on Furness Abbey's land, but to which the Abbey now granted formal status, and a hundred years later the bloomery (iron ore smelter) at Cunsey on the western side of Windermere contracted to buy all the trees on Hacket Ground for use in charcoal making.

Follow the lane west from Stang End as it twists and turns above the Brathay. Ignore the bridge leading to a lane north of the river and keep to the south bank, but after another three hundred yards take a path along the bank as far as Slater Bridge. This is a delightful footbridge consisting of slate slabs crossing the Brathay with the help of a small island, and was originally built by workers employed in the many quarries scarring the face of Wetherlam which fills the southern horizon with its broad flanks. It will certainly also have been used by Lanty Slee, a nineteenth-century whisky smuggler whose stills were located in caves on the slopes of Wetherlam and in the Tilberthwaite Fells, and much of whose whisky was taken across the Wrynose and Hardknott passes to the old port of Ravenglass. Often prosecuted but never tempted to give up his illicit distilling, Lanty Slee died in 1878, at the age of seventy-six, at Greenbank Farm, a few steps up the Skelwith road from The Three Shires Inn.

Cross the Brathay on Slater Bridge, incline right through a gateway and use the track climbing steadily across fields, flanked by little outcrops of bright rock, to reach a minor lane. Turn left here, past some cottages, to join the main valley road just to the east of the little chapel and just west of The Three Shires Inn, noted for its bar food and, more recently, its real draught beer. The chapel, which was in ruins in 1692, was last restored in 1866 and was also used as a school until 1905, when a separate schoolroom and teacher's house were provided. There is not much more to the hamlet of **Little Langdale** than this, although there are a few cottages straggling along the road, some farms – including Wilson's Place, a name more reminiscent of Great Langdale – and one or two new houses which have somehow satisfied the very strict planning controls in force throughout the National Park. The best feature of the hamlet is probably the view across the Brathay valley and Little Langdale Tarn to the noble peak of Wetherlam, and then westwards towards Wrynose Pass, the next target of the Roman Way.

4 WRYNOSE AND HARDKNOTT
Little Langdale to Boot (11 miles/18km)

Leave the hamlet of Little Langdale along the motor road heading for Wrynose Pass; in summer there will almost certainly be a stream of cars travelling the same way, and quite possibly a tailback caused by the inexperience or incompetence of a driver who has underestimated the difficulties of the road ahead. For the first mile the road is really the only option for westbound travellers (a long detour round by Slater Bridge and Low Hall Garth cuts out more than half of the dull trudge but does add to the time and effort required). Over on the left, in a shallow basin, is **Little Langdale Tarn**, one of the least memorable of the larger sheets of water in the Lake District. All the excitement in the Brathay valley occurs downstream, especially at Colwith Force, and the tarn is merely a shallow, reed-fringed pool, distinguished only by the large number of streams which feed it.

Continue past the junction with the Blea Tarn road (another favourite spot for motorised lunacy) and swing round a right-hand bend with the farm at **Fell Foot** directly ahead. The low,

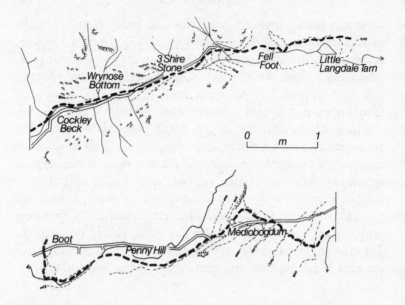

white farmhouse and its yews, the curious terraced mound behind it and the rocky bluff of Castle Howe to the right make an attractive composition. The farmhouse doubled as an inn when the packhorse (and smuggling) trade over Wrynose was at its height.

It has been claimed that the strange terraced earthwork behind the farm, with its steep sides, flat top and approximately rectangular shape, was a 'thing-mount', the place where the Viking settlers of the two Langdales held their annual parliament, although there is little evidence to support the assertion. At least Castle Howe, craggily guarding the way up to the pass, is natural enough, and the minor scramble to its summit is rewarded with a fine view north towards the Langdale Pikes, as well as a second look, this time from above, at the strange mound of Fell Foot.

The fields of Fell Foot farm are the last signs of cultivation for several miles, and this brings two advantages. First, the line of the Roman road, its course now uncluttered by later development, can still be deduced in places. Secondly, the detective work involved in tracing its course takes the walker away from the busy metalled road and onto green paths through the bracken. The first of these excellent escape routes starts near the Pedder Stone, a prominent boulder south of the road, and keeps to the edge of the steep ground below Hollin Crag, just on the other side of the road. The Roman road kept to this route as far as Wrynose Bridge.

The path crosses Wrynose Beck, one of the main feeders of the River Brathay, a hundred yards above the road bridge, curves round below Green Crag, rejoins the present road and then bears slightly left just before the **Three Shire Stone**, the unexceptional stone pillar which previously marked the boundary between Lancashire (the only county named on the pillar, which is inscribed 'Lancashire, W.F. 1816'), Cumberland and Westmorland at the summit of Wrynose Pass, 1,281ft above sea level. The purpose of the pillar disappeared with local government reorganisation in 1974.

It is worth reflecting on the fact that prior to the Second World War the road over Wrynose was unsurfaced, and it was only the deterioration of the surface caused by army training vehicles which caused it to be improved, largely with concrete at first and later with tarmac. The ascent of the pass, on a steep, narrow and tortuous road, is one of the most testing problems faced on English roads, and indeed in winter the road is often closed for long periods because of drifting snow. Only the proximity of Hardknott Pass, an even stiffer obstacle, prevents Wrynose from achieving the notoriety it deserves.

Westward from the Three Shire Stone the Roman road lies south of the tarmac road for some distance, but then recrosses it and in **Wrynose Bottom** it remains to the north of both the River Duddon and the present road. The approximate line of the Roman road is shown as a public right of way on the Ordnance Survey map (though the path on the ground is not so unerringly straight as it appears on the map), and it can be followed all the way to Cockley Beck Bridge, the last half mile being an excellent riverside walk along by the Duddon. The Roman road in Wrynose Bottom has been shown to be some twenty feet wide in certain places, emphasising its importance to the Romans as a defensive measure in these hostile fells.

The course of the Roman road is known fairly accurately between **Cockley Beck** and the fort of Hardknott, and it is possible to follow it on paths which form a splendid alternative to the motor road over Hardknott Pass, a particularly difficult drive and one which is often congested in summer. Having crossed Mosedale Beck and arrived at the Eskdale road immediately west of Cockley Beck Bridge, press on straight ahead along the track parallel to the River Duddon as far as the youth hostel at Black Hall. Beyond the youth hostel leave this track (which heads down Dunnerdale) to the right and strike up a path which chooses a careful zigzag course to the top of Hardknott Pass, 1,291ft above sea level.

This was an ingenious solution to the problem of getting a road up the steep side of the pass, but Roman ingenuity did not end there. On the way up from the Duddon valley clever use is made of cuttings and terracing to ease the average gradient, and below Raven Crag a cutting 15ft deep and 15ft wide has been driven through the lower buttresses of the crag. The Roman road coincides with the motor road for a short distance west of the summit of Hardknott Pass, but then follows a path which swings away north-west through the bracken below the minor crags of Border End to reach a grassy shelf where the slope eases on the generally steep and rough south-western spur of the low fell of Hard Knott. This shelf was selected by the Romans as the site of their garrison fort of **Mediobogdum**, now generally known as Hardknott Castle. The remains of the fort, now in the care of the Department of the Environment, are substantial and a detailed exploration is well worth while.

Approaching from the east, the first evidence of Roman occupation is a square of smooth, level ground with a raised area on one side forming an inspection platform. This was the parade ground, about three acres in extent, an oasis of green surrounded by a chaotic landscape of tumbled boulders. Even though its site was carefully chosen to take advantage of the gentle slope here, it was still necessary to excavate to lower the eastern side and raise the southern and western edges and therefore achieve an acceptably flat space. The parade ground was linked by a rough road to the fort itself, in its astonishing position on a spur between the valleys of the River Esk and Hardknott Gill, and overlooking Eskdale as far as the Irish Sea at Ravenglass.

The fort covers about three acres, and appears to have been constructed between 117 and 138 AD. There is some evidence to suggest that the fort was fully garrisoned with a complete regiment for only a short period – the commandant's house was not completed on such a lavish scale as was first contemplated, and the bath-house south of the fort was too small to serve a full garrison. Despite the wild grandeur of its setting, in an almost impregnable position high above the Esk valley, Hardknott served no great strategic purpose in the defence of Roman Britain and it was probably abandoned as early as 250 AD.

The fort adhered to the standard Roman plan, with an internal tower at each corner of a square walled enclosure and a gateway in the centre of each wall. This led to the oddity of the northern gate leading directly to the top of a crag dropping steeply into Eskdale, an indication, perhaps, of inflexibility and single-mindedness of purpose. The stone for the entrance gates was a red sandstone imported ten miles or so from Gosforth, but the rougher masonry is of local origin. The walls have been sensitively restored by the Department of the Environment, the stone below the narrow slate course being original and that above the slate slabs having been reconstructed from fallen masonry. Only the major internal buildings – the commandant's house, 'principia' or headquarters, and granaries which could hold enough grain to supply a regiment of five hundred men for two years – were built of stone, and the barracks and less important buildings were made of timber.

To the south, outside the fort itself, are the remains of the bath-house, a small and fairly simple arrangement of cold plunge (frigidarium), warm bath (tepidarium) and hot bath (caldarium). The furnace, built of brick, was next to the latter so that the hot bath would obtain most of the heat. Glance back from the baths to see the fort itself in perspective, with the main gateway in the centre of the nearest (southern) wall, and the highest land in

Harter Fell
from Doctor Bridge, Eskdale

England seemingly a stone's throw away across the Esk valley. No wonder this has been described as one of the most outstanding Roman sites in Britain.

Leave the Roman fort on the track leading south-west and rejoin the motor road for part of its hazardous descent into the Esk valley. Away to the right lies the noble seventeenth-century farmhouse of Brotherilkeld, start of the second leg of the Lakeland Horseshoe, which travels upstream along the Esk and then climbs Scafell Pike and Scafell. The remainder of today's walk is less strenuous but no less attractive, since it is soon possible to escape from the busy surfaced road and use the old packhorse route via Penny Hill Farm to St Catherine's Chapel on the river bank south of Boot. At the foot of Hardknott Pass the first cultivated land since Fell Foot (apart from the few fields at Cockley Beck) is encountered, and the line of the Roman road is uncertain, but the Penny Hill lane is of some antiquity and may well represent the approximate route.

After leaving the tarmac road, fork right (the main track leads to Seathwaite in Dunnerdale) after some two hundred yards, keeping close to a patch of woodland, and traverse the lower slopes of Harter Fell on a gradually improving path. Harter Fell, which stands in isolation from the major groups of fells, has the real feel of a mountain about it and has an exquisite rock tor of a summit; the route to the top from Boot is a succession of delights. The path around its base is less eventful, but has some fine close-up views of the fast-flowing River Esk and eventually reaches the farm buildings at **Penny Hill**.

Across the valley is The Woolpack Inn, built, as its name suggests, to serve the packhorse trains using Hardknott, the only route east out of Eskdale. Ironically the packhorse trade which prompted the construction of the inn began to decline soon after it was opened, and only the modern tourist trade has come to the rescue of the pub. What is less well known is that the predecessor of The Woolpack, an inn called The Pyet's Nest, was situated here at Penny Hill. Continue westwards from the old farm to reach the river at Doctor Bridge, a splendid high, single-arched, granite bridge spanning the rocky bed of the Esk;

Doctor Bridge.

keep to the south bank of the river past Low Birker until just
before Birker Beck is reached, turning right to cross the river on
massive stepping stones and reach the chapel of St Catherine.

There was a chapel on this secluded riverside site as long ago as
the fourteenth century, and the present tiny building, with a
combined nave and chancel and a slender bell-cote, is probably
little changed in style from the original. Severely simple but
unquestionably an integral part of the scene, it is a typical dale
chapel. The churchyard contains the grave of Tommy Dobson,
who founded the Eskdale and Ennerdale Farmers Hunt in 1857,
and whose grave has carvings of a hound, a fox and the
celebrated huntsman himself. Only a short walk away from the
river, along a narrow lane, is the main valley road and the hamlet
of **Boot**, the starting point of the Valley Route.

5 LOWER ESKDALE TO THE SEA
Boot to Ravenglass (8 miles/13km)

Leave Boot by retracing your steps down to the chapel of St

Catherine, cross the river and, on reaching the track heading down the valley, turn right and then quickly left to climb up the ravine of Stanley Gill as far as Dalegarth Force (also known as Stanley Force), one of the finest waterfalls in the Lake District. Its situation, in a deep, precipitously steep-sided and richly wooded ravine is tremendous, and the waterfall itself issues over a rock step directly into a pool some sixty feet below. The woodland and cliffs of Stanley Gill have now become the setting for an excellent nature walk, with the waterfall as its highlight; indeed the only disappointment is the tendency for the gill, by no means a major tributary of the Esk, to produce only a thin trickle of water to plunge over the lip of the force.

Return to the track and turn down the valley, passing on the right Dalegarth Hall, a manor house distinguished by the round chimneys more usually found in the former county of Westmorland than in west Cumberland. It was called Austhwaite Hall in the twelfth century, but came into the Stanley family through marriage two centuries later, and remained their home for about

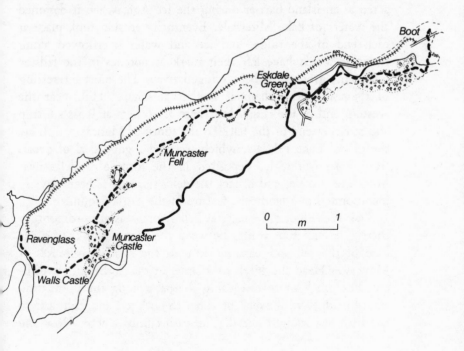

three hundred years, until they moved to Ponsonby, north of Gosforth on the Cumberland plain. The house was fortified around 1450, with a pele tower added, but much of the structure was demolished in the eighteenth century, only to be restored later. One survival is the plaster ceiling, which dates from 1599.

Beyond Dalegarth Hall the Roman Way passes through well-wooded and sometimes quite marshy country close to the River Esk (Milkingstead Mire is a significant placename around here) and then reaches a metalled road just south of Forge Bridge, after a delightfully quiet two-mile walk from Boot. A short distance across the bridge is The King George IV, a pleasant pub which was called the King of Prussia until 1914, when it was felt prudent to change the name. Just before **Eskdale Green** station on the Ravenglass & Eskdale narrow-gauge railway take the bridleway heading left away from the road towards Bankend Wood and Muncaster Fell.

This low, narrow but fascinating fell, with its corrugated summit ridge, is of particular interest to geologists because it acted as an island barrier during the Ice Age, when it dammed the waters of Lake Miterdale. Eventually erosion took place at each end of the ridge, and ice and water overflowed along channels which have left their mark as notches in the fellside where the granite has been gouged away. The most interesting of these overflow channels is that at Chapel Hill, near the western end of the ridge, but there are others at Ross's Camp and at either end of the fell. To the south of Muncaster Fell lay the glacial Lake Eskdale, which received a good deal of debris from Lake Miterdale, deposited in the form of a delta near Muncaster Castle, and in fact the delta terrace has been cleverly incorporated as a landscape feature in the castle grounds.

Back at the foot of Muncaster Fell's north-eastern promontory there is a choice of routes between the easy path skirting the base of the fell and passing close to the solid farmhouses at Muncaster Head and High Eskholme, or the slightly more difficult but much more rewarding footpath along the undulating summit ridge, with excellent views to both left and right and to the Irish Sea straight ahead. The path climbs Rabbit How and

Pele Tower
Muncaster Castle

meanders across to Ross's Camp, a popular picnic spot with the
odd outcrop adding colour to the scene, then avoids the highest
point of **Muncaster Fell** (a mere 758ft above sea level) and
reaches Chapel Hill, named after the chapels on its southern flank
but most notable for a tarn, with three islands, which occupies
the floor of the glacial overflow channel, and the strange late
eighteenth-century monument, a squat three-storey tower with

an octagonal spire, on a spur above Chapel Wood.

There is now a very gradual descent down to the main Barrow to Workington road (A595) at a very sharp bend. Another bridleway heads roughly north at this point, and can be used if, on this very easy final day, an extra mile or so of walking is desired in order to visit Muncaster Mill, which was restored to working order in the 1970s. The mill operated continuously until 1954 and has therefore suffered only a short break in operation. It is known to have been working in 1470, although the present structure is less than two hundred years old. Corn was milled until 1914, and then oatmeal and cattle feed for the next forty years. Now the mill, with its 13ft overshot wheel, produces wholemeal flour, and visitors can see the whole process in operation. It also has its own halt on the narrow-gauge railway, but Roman Way walkers will surely not be tempted by this and will hurry back to the main road at the base of Muncaster Fell.

A short walk along the road is inevitable, in the direction of Barrow, but this is followed by a walk through the grounds of **Muncaster Castle**. The chief attribute of the castle itself is its commanding position above the Esk valley, since the building is essentially no more than a Victorian country house, constructed in 1862–6 for the fourth Lord Muncaster. It was, however, built onto a medieval pele tower (the north-west tower is a Victorian addition). The castle has been owned by the Pennington family since the thirteenth century, and houses an extensive collection of antique furniture.

The special feature of Muncaster Castle, however, is the superb array of landscaped gardens, and in particular the famous Terrace Walk, developed on the delta terrace of the glacial lake already described. The gardens are at their best in late May and early June, when the azaleas and rhododendrons are in full bloom and the effect, with Muncaster Fell immediately behind and the pale blue line of the Eskdale fells in the distance, is really spectacular. Like many stately homes, Muncaster has had to provide new attractions in order to survive, and the peaceful atmosphere is somewhat diluted by the adventure playground.

Walls Castle

A footpath leads past the pele tower and the later additions forming the present Muncaster Castle and passes through Dovecot Wood before proceeding roughly south-west to the cluster of buildings at Newtown. Keep to the right here, then fork left to arrive at what little remains of the Roman fort of Glannaventa. The indications are that the fort (its name can be translated as 'the town on the bank') covered about four acres and faced inland, protecting the road rather than the harbour. There would also appear to have been an extensive civil settlement outside the north gate. Very little can be seen today, however, since part of the site lies in the woods and a great deal of the remainder was fairly comprehensively demolished when the railway was cut through the site in the nineteenth century.

Much more interesting are the remains of the bath-house, rather confusingly called **Walls Castle**, which lie to the north of the fort. The walls stand to a height of ten or twelve feet, making this the tallest surviving Roman building in northern Britain, and its survival is all the more remarkable given its history of abandonment and decay. Yet the condition of the walls, and of the pinkish mortar used in rendering them internally, is in some places excellent, and it is easy to pick out the main features of the design, with doorways, windows and even little niches in the walls indicating four rooms including a changing room, an anteroom and the baths themselves.

Inevitably this unusual building, the true purpose of which was not immediately recognised when it was rediscovered, has drawn to itself a number of legends, mainly relating to the uses to which it has been put since the time of the Romans. It has been suggested that the Penningtons pressed Walls Castle into service as their manor house before moving slightly up the hill to Muncaster, and that it served as a leper hospital, but there is little evidence to support these theories. The same is true of the legend that this was the castle of Eveling or Avallach, the Celtic lord of the underworld.

Keep to the track northwards from Walls Castle as it progresses along the eastern edge of Walls Plantation. The wood and the railway combine to restrict the view to the left over the sand dunes to the estuary of the River Esk, but eventually a minor road is encountered at the end of the wood. Turn left here, pass under the bridge carrying the narrow-gauge railway towards Eskdale and then under the main line railway, and turn the corner (at which the route fording the estuary of the River Mite to Saltcoats, only a practical proposition at low tide, joins from the north) to enter the single street of **Ravenglass**. Merely a small village these days, Ravenglass has had a long and remarkable history, and this failed market town and former busy port, which first grew as the successor to the Roman settlement only a few hundred yards away, is a worthy final objective of the Roman Way.

The greater importance of the place in the past is evidenced by its wide market street. The first market charter was granted in 1209, and the Saturday market and annual fair were clearly highly successful when the port was busy and trade with Ireland was substantial. As late as 1675 the fair lasted for three days, with cattle, sheep and other goods changing hands, and a general air of hard bargaining and gentle lawlessness. The reputation of Ravenglass as a refuge for villains, and especially smugglers, lasted well beyond their demise.

Shortly after 1675 the market and fair began to go into

decline, and a century later the place was in decay. Lord Muncaster attempted to inject renewed life by obtaining a new charter in 1796 for two markets each week and three annual fairs, but their success was shortlived and the second half of the nineteenth century saw the fortunes of Ravenglass once more at a low ebb. The fairs had been discontinued and the weekly markets were small and poorly attended. Nowadays Ravenglass Fair is held in Signal Box Field each May, but it is a concoction for tourists rather than a true Cumbrian country gathering.

Nevertheless, Ravenglass is now a highly attractive coastal village, with its single street leading almost to the water's edge. Along the street, which is continuously built up and thus possesses a deceptively urban feel, are the early Victorian Methodist chapel, a succession of well-maintained and often whitewashed town cottages, a slight increase in the width of the street where the former market cross stood and (most urban of all) signs to the railway station. The northbound platform houses The Ratty Arms, converted from redundant station buildings into an enterprising free house. At its southern end the main street fades away as it approaches yet another meander loop of the Esk estuary. The harbour has virtually gone, the channel having gradually silted up, but there are still some boats (some can be hired by the day for sea fishing) and fresh fish is still sold direct from the trawler on the beach.

Ravenglass stands right in the middle of the sandy estuaries of the Esk, Mite and Irt, protected from westerly winds by lines of sand dunes, and the same dune systems are the home of the Drigg Dunes nature reserve and gullery, which has one of the most important breeding colonies of the greater black-headed gull in Europe, together with four species of tern. (A permit is required to visit the nature reserve.) The mudflats are the territory of several varieties of wading birds, and this quiet sanctuary has also become a popular picnic place, so far without detriment to the wildlife.

The gentle landscape of Cumbria's western coast, with its small and quiet-flowing rivers and low sandhills, may seem an incongruous end to the Roman journey from the outskirts of

Penrith across the high fells of the High Street system and over the Wrynose and Hardknott passes into Eskdale. Yet the scant remains of the fort near Ravenglass symbolise, just as much as the more spectacular example of Hardknott Castle, the determination of the Romans to impress their rule on this remote area of highland Britain, a determination which first created the Roman Way.

THE NORTH-WESTERN FELLS

It would not be difficult to argue that the north-western fells present the finest short introduction to the delights of the Lakeland mountains. Within their boundaries they include superb high-level ridge walks, such as those radiating from Dale Head, together with the grandeur of Eel Crag and the Grasmoor group of fells, and the charm of the Catbells ridge. This two-day walk links the best of these contrasting attractions in a short but nevertheless quite challenging expedition. On both days the initial stages of the walk are similar to parts of the Lakeland Horseshoe, and so – purely to avoid repetition – the route descriptions are rather shorter than normal. This should certainly not be taken as indicating that this excellent excursion is somehow less worthy than the others!

1 THE CATBELLS RIDGE AND ROBINSON
Keswick to Buttermere via Dale Head
(13 miles/21km)

The first part of this walk reverses the route followed by the fourth stage of the Lakeland Horseshoe, and fuller details will be found there. From the Moot Hall in Keswick, walk down to the bridge over the River Greta and take the footpath over the fields and across the River Derwent to the village of Portinscale. Head south along the road signposted to the Newlands valley, but just beyond Derwent Bank look for a footpath on the left, which snakes through woodland across the drive leading to **Lingholm**, with its fine gardens, and on to Silver Hill. Copperheap Bay, down on the left on the shores of **Derwentwater**, owes its

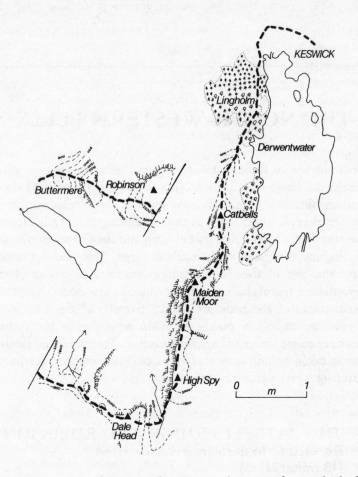

The map shows locations including KESWICK, Lingholm, Derwentwater, Buttermere, Robinson ▲, Catbells ▲, Maiden Moor ▲, High Spy ▲, and Dale Head ▲, with a scale bar marked 0 m 1.

curious name to the time when it was the point from which the ore from the prolific mines at Goldscope and Dale Head was taken across the lake to the smelter at Brigham on the outskirts of Keswick.

The path is now signposted as far as the road at Hawse End. Follow the road around an uphill zigzag, then bear right onto the very well-used path ascending the northern slopes of Catbells. This is an easy climb, yet is really enchanting, with superb views of the fells across Derwentwater. When the summit of the northern spur is reached, there follows a fine stroll along the undulating ridge to the highest point of **Catbells**

(1,481ft). The view is tremendous, with Skiddaw and Blencathra prominent across Derwentwater, the Helvellyn range seen behind the lower fells on the far side of Borrowdale and, to the south-east, a fine picture of the Newlands fells.

Down below, on the eastern slopes of Catbells, is Brandlehow Park, which was in 1902 the first acquisition of the fledgeling National Trust, and at least until recently was one of the last refuges of the red squirrel. (A mile or so south is Manesty where the Trust scored a notable victory in 1908 by acquiring land which had already been marked out as building plots.) At the southern tip of the wooded Brandlehow Park are the rather less attractive remains of the largest and most ancient of the Borrowdale lead mines. The lead veins run roughly north–south below the slopes of Catbells, but when the higher veins were worked out the lower outcrops, down by the lake shore, proved impossible to work successfully, despite their high quality, because of the problems of drainage.

The mine was reopened in the nineteenth century by the Keswick Mining Company, who erected a waterwheel 30ft in diameter and driven by steam pumps to drain the workings. For a time this was successful, and up to three hundred tons a year of good-quality lead ore was extracted, with eighty men employed. The waterwheel was an unusual attraction for the tourists who were now beginning to discover Borrowdale, but by 1864 it was proving unequal to the task of keeping the faces free of water and the mine was finally abandoned. Today its scars, in the form of spoil heaps, are overgrown and relatively unobtrusive.

Back on the ridge, aim south from the summit of Catbells towards the col at Hause Gate, where the path from Newlands to Grange-in-Borrowdale crosses the broad ridge path. To the left, towards the bottom of the slope, is Brackenburn, one of the homes of Sir Hugh Walpole from 1924 until his death in 1941. Walpole drew inspiration from the Borrowdale landscape for the Herries novels, set in Watendlath and in and around the Catbells area. He is buried in St John's churchyard in Keswick, in a spot looking across the lake to Catbells.

Take the obvious path climbing the ridge south from Hause

Gate, with the broken crags of Trap Knotts forming an effective
foreground for the glimpse along the valley of Newlands Beck.
The path rises to a prominent cairn on the edge of the summit
plateau – there is an exquisite view from here of the southern
face of Blencathra across the wide expanse of Derwentwater –
then steers a course above the rim of Bull Crag to the grassy
summit of **Maiden Moor** (1,887ft). Across Newlands can be seen
the site of the Goldscope mine, above Low Snab on the shoulder
of Scope End. A very rich vein of copper 9ft thick was being
mined here in the thirteenth century, together with lead and
small quantities of silver and possibly gold. Goldscope's greatest
period of productivity began in 1561, when the Society for the
Mines Royal was formed and German miners were specifically
brought in to exploit the Newlands mines. The mine closed but
was reopened in 1847; it was producing over three hundred tons
of lead a year in the 1850s, yet it had been abandoned by the end
of the next decade.

Head south across the flat, grassy plateau on the top of
Maiden Moor, keeping to the path as the ridge narrows near
Blea Crag and then rises to the summit of **High Spy** (2,143ft).
This is a relatively unknown mountain, although the mile-long
wall of Eel Crags which guards its Newlands flank is quite an
important rock-climbing area. The level summit is long and
fairly narrow, quite rocky and adorned at its highest point with a
bulky cairn. Continue along the ridge, still bearing roughly
south, and descend by the path keeping just to the east of Eel
Crags to the col at Rigg Head.

The area around Rigg Head is at best marshy and after heavy
rain can be distinctly difficult to cross in an even temper. On the
far side of the stream is Dalehead Tarn, small and disappointing.
Beyond the tarn there is the weary necessity of regaining the
height lost in the long descent from High Spy, either by a frontal
attack up the fellside or by aiming south-west, at first along the
beck and later obliquely up the steep slopes to pick up the track
coming up from Honister.

The reward for all this exertion is the satisfaction of having
scaled **Dale Head** (2,473ft), the highest of the fells in the

triangle between Newlands Hause, Honister Pass and Borrow-dale. It is not a mountain which immediately strikes one as impressive, yet it has qualities which give it prominence among the north-western fells. It has dramatic crags, a fine summit perched on the end of a splendid ridge and, most of all, it commands a spectacular view straight down Newlands, the dale which it dominates and from which it gained its name.

The actual summit is not in doubt, close to the fell's northern precipice of Dalehead Crags. Whether there is a cairn will depend on the state of play between wreckers and rebuilders, for this, like the summit cairn on Pike of Blisco and Robinson's Cairn on Pillar, is one of the cairns to have attracted the attention of vandals. The original tall, slim, slate pillar has long since gone, but its successors are (while they last) almost equally worthy and they mark a place with an exceptional panorama. Not only is there the chance to look straight along Newlands, between the spurs of Hindscarth and High Spy, to the hamlet of Little Town and the wooded hills around Swinside, there is also the long blue line of the Helvellyn range, the distant peaks around Bowfell and Scafell Pike, the bulky outline of Pillar and, across Hindscarth, the Grasmoor fells, each adding their own distinctive contribution to the scene.

Below the craggy northern face of Dale Head there was another mining venture. The Dale Head copper mines were first worked by the Germans in the sixteenth century, though later the Duke of Somerset took over the operation and built a bloomery to process the ore, which had previously been smelted lower down the valley at Stonycroft. The ruined sheds still remain, together with the spoil heaps, where some of the stones contain bright-green copper malachite veins.

The ridge west from Dale Head forms the next stage of the walk, and indeed it is one of the highlights. Pleasantly rocky and in places quite narrow, it has superlative views. The path skirts a deep gully before rising over rocks and improving into a broad path following a line of ruined fenceposts. The deep bowl of the Buttermere valley lies below the ridge to the west, with the eroded flank of Red Pike prominent beyond the lake. After about

Robinson

a mile the path along the ridge reaches a large cairn which marks
the divergence of the route to Hindscarth, a worth-while
divergence unless time is short, since the detour takes only about
fifteen minutes. Beyond this point the route skirts the head of
Little Dale, a wet and unfrequented side valley, on its way to
Robinson, which is reached up a simple and mainly grassy slope.

Robinson (2,417ft), despite its drab name, is a sturdy and distinctive member of the group of fells ringing the head of Newlands, although the Buttermere side of the mountain is admittedly less exciting. The name derives, rather unromantically, from an early landowner. The summit is flat, quite stony and distinguished by two low rock outcrops which snake across the top of the fell. A small cairn denotes the top, but there is little else to see and nothing to warrant any delay before the final part of the day's walk, the descent to Buttermere, is undertaken.

The first part of the descent is perfectly straightforward, since a line of cairns indicates the path as it runs south-west across the plateau and down the pleasant, occasionally rocky, upper slopes. However, just below a sheepfold the character of the walk changes fundamentally as Buttermere Moss is encountered. This is a sphagnum bog situated on a shelf jutting out from the bulky western shoulder of Robinson, and it can be particularly difficult and even dangerous in wet weather. Over the years it has built up a formidable reputation, no doubt partly apocryphal, and there are stories of horses having been lost in the peaty morass. Certainly walkers have been known to sink into waist-deep mud after straying from the only recommended route through the bog.

This recommended route follows the line of an old sledgate, a track originally made for bringing down peat from the Moss. The green track had a foundation of boulders and was covered in turf, but has long since deteriorated and some parts are in disrepair. In wet weather, or even in mist, other more circuitous routes from Robinson to Buttermere (perhaps via Newlands Hause) are worth considering, but otherwise the long struggle through the marsh, with its many small pools, is likely to have a successful outcome. The way then lies over the shoulder of High Snockrigg, which has an excellent prospect over the Buttermere valley, and down over loose, slaty rocks above the ravine at the head of Near Broken Gill, to reach an easy path heading through the bracken to the road from Newlands to Buttermere.

Only a few hundred yards walking now remain, but there is

Buttermere

no reason to hurry. Ahead is the peaceful lake of Buttermere, backed by the steep slopes of the High Stile fells, and with the tremendous cascade of Sourmilk Gill escaping over the lip of the hanging valley which contains Bleaberry Tarn. In front of the lake, though half hidden in the trees, is the village of **Buttermere**, and closer still is the attractive little dale chapel perched above the village. The road from Newlands dips steeply down past the chapel, joins the valley road, and drops down into the village, with its café and two hotels strategically situated at the end of a long and varied day on the north-western fells.

2 THE GRASMOOR GROUP
Buttermere to Keswick via Grisedale Pike
(11 miles/18km)

The first section of this walk, as far as Grasmoor, follows the route selected by the Lakeland Horseshoe over Whiteless Pike to Thirdgill Head Man, and so only a summary of its main features is given here. There is a possible alternative way to the top of

Grasmoor, using the footpath down Rannerdale and then ascending the spur of Lad Hows and the narrow ridge linking it to its parent fell, but this is longer and involves slightly more climbing, and the classic Whiteless Pike route is to be preferred.

From Buttermere take the Sail Pass track from Crag Houses, but quickly turn left to ascend the shoulder of Whiteless Pike, pausing only to enjoy the retrospective vista over the Buttermere valley. The small, neat summit of **Whiteless Pike** (2,159ft) defends the western end of a high and narrow ridge between two deep valleys. The ridge is followed to Thirdgill Head Man but then, instead of following the course of the Lakeland Horseshoe to Wandope, keep straight on across the wide sheepwalk in the direction of Coledale Hause. Well before the hause turn left at a cairn close to some pools in a shallow depression and approach the summit of **Grasmoor** (2,791ft) by following a line of cairns over the grassy tableland.

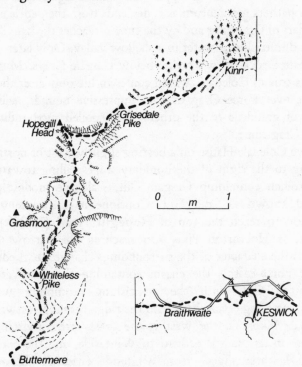

This is in some ways a disappointing route, at least from Thirdgill Head Man onwards, to the top of the highest of the north-western fells. Yet there is little alternative from Buttermere, for Grasmoor's crags and rocky bluffs face north and east, and can only really be tackled from the northern end of Crummock Water. Nevertheless, the top bastions of the crags forming Grasmoor End can quickly be discovered west of the summit and, after savouring the excellent panorama available from the cairn, the rim of Dove Crags can be followed down to Coledale Hause, where the track from Lanthwaite Green to Braithwaite is crossed.

Coledale Hause is virtually surrounded by fine mountains – Grasmoor, Eel Crag, Grisedale Pike and Hopegill Head – and looks out over the dramatic rocky valleys of Gasgale Gill and Coledale Beck. Yet the place itself is merely a desolate expanse of grass above the marshy upper valley of Gasgale Gill, which slowly gathers momentum as it descends from the gentle eastern shoulders of Grasmoor and by the time it reaches the hause is still only a thin trickle of water in a shallow valley. Only later does it dominate a rock-strewn ravine below Gasgale Crags. Much the same is true of Coledale, which comes to life only after the beck crashes over Force Crag in two impressive bounds, adding a touch of grandeur to the otherwise despoiled surroundings of Force Crag mine.

Leave Coledale Hause on a bearing slightly west of north and, keeping to the right of the bouldery slopes falling towards the deep trench containing Gasgale Gill, scale the modest grassy mound known as Sand Hill. Continue in the same general direction to reach the top of **Hopegill Head** (2,525ft), also known as Hobcarton Pike. On reaching the narrow, rocky summit the character of the surroundings changes markedly, for to the north-east is the chasm containing the headwaters of Hobcarton Gill, with the astonishing crumbling wall of Hobcarton Crag eating back into the ridge running eastwards to Grisedale Pike. To the west is the grassy arête twisting and turning on its gradual descent to Whiteside, and the combination of the three ridges – from Whiteside, Grisedale Pike and the

The Grasmoor Group

outlier of Ladyside Pike to the north – has left Hopegill Head with a small and graceful summit spectacularly perched directly above Hope Gill.

The bulk of Grasmoor and Eel Crag, the markedly higher fells just beyond Gasgale Gill and Coledale Hause, restricts the range of fells which can be seen from the neat summit of Hopegill Head, although beyond Whiteside to the west is the coastal plain and, round to the north, the Solway Firth, while the line of the Helvellyn massif is reassuringly present to the east. The Skiddaw fells, though, seem curiously misshapen, and Blencathra is uncharacteristically shy. To the north the eye is attracted along the line of Ladyside Pike towards the Vale of Lorton and the distant slate roofs of the town of Cockermouth.

The walk takes the track skirting round above the impressive wall of shattered slate forming Hobcarton Crag, aiming for Grisedale Pike. The crag is an extraordinary sight, a bleak wall in dull weather but a colourful mixture of heather, bilberry and splintered blue-grey slate in sunshine. There are two tremendous gullies and a number of rock towers, distinctly unsafe in their position at the crest of a sheer face falling to the coniferous forest which cloaks the side valley of Hobcarton Gill. The steepness of the crag, its dangerous condition (which puts it decisively out of bounds for rock climbers) and a geological oddity, a quartz band in the Skiddaw Slates which is unusually rich in pyrites, have combined to provide the ideal conditions for one of only two British locations in which the red alpine catchfly flourishes. Even the sheep cannot reach its hiding place high up on the treacherous rock, let alone 'collectors'.

The path continues above the crag, then picks up the line of a ruined stone wall and follows this up over some pleasantly angled slabs of Skiddaw Slate and then over loose, shaly scree to the summit of **Grisedale Pike** (2,593ft). This is a mountain which, when seen from a distance, arrests the walker's attention because of its finely proportioned pyramidal summit rising from broad fellsides. On closer inspection the same walker is unlikely to be disappointed, since the summit cairn is defiantly perched on a slate outcrop at a point where the ridge is very narrow and extremely stony. This is an appropriately rough but attractive top to a classic Lakeland mountain.

It is interesting to compare the view from Grisedale Pike with that from nearby Hopegill Head, but it will probably be some time before this exercise is attempted, since all eyes will first of all be focused on the startling wall of Hobcarton Crag falling for some five hundred feet below Hopegill Head. The crag has become a familiar object on this section of the journey, yet it is still an arresting sight. The rest of the panorama is equally impressive, as befits this excellent mountain. Swinging left from Hopegill Head, the highlights include the great eastern buttress of Grasmoor, then Eel Crag – especially impressive from this angle, which emphasises the rough, broken cliff which lends its name to the fell – the Newlands fells with Bowfell and Scafell behind, Helvellyn across Derwentwater, Blencathra (again, as from Hopegill Head, curiously truncated and failing to impose the grandeur of its serrated southern profile on the scene), Skiddaw beyond Bassenthwaite Lake, and the Vale of Lorton and Cumbrian coastline to the north.

The northern foreground is largely composed of conifers, for this is the area around Whinlatter Pass where the Forestry Commission's first planting in the Lake District took place. Planting began in 1919 in Hospital Plantation (named after the former isolation hospital, now a private house, on the north-eastern slopes of Grisedale Pike) and in the aftermath of the First World War the need for timber was the only consideration. The result was a sterile and regimented approach with no regard to the effect on the Lakeland landscape. Uniform rows of Sitka spruce throttled the life out of the valleys of Hobcarton Gill and Grisedale Gill, and on the intervening spurs planting took place up to 1,700ft – so close to the valuable asset of Hobcarton Crag, in fact, that in a rare incursion into this area the National Trust stepped in to buy the most valuable part of the cliff and the scree-ridden area around its base.

Since those early days there has, of course, been a marked change for the better in Forestry Commission attitudes, and now that much of the first crop from the Whinlatter plantations has been or shortly will be harvested, there is an opportunity to put the new, more enlightened approach into effect, with amenity planting and greater freedom to walk in the forests. Hospital Plantation and its neighbours now form part of Thornthwaite Forest, with a visitor centre close to the summit of Whinlatter Pass and car parks, forest trails and picnic sites provided for car-borne tourists.

The next objective is the village of Braithwaite, which can be seen nestling beneath the eastern shoulder of Grisedale Pike. It is quite easy to go astray in the first few yards, for the apparently obvious path leading away from the summit cairn in fact heads for the north-east ridge and the Whinlatter plantations. The Braithwaite path bears away to the right of this, over shaly stones onto the narrow and initially quite steep eastern arête, the feature which is so prominent from around Keswick. Eventually the slope eases and the journey becomes more comfortable on the heather- and bilberry-covered ridge of Sleet How. Below to the left is Grisedale, at the head of which Grisedale Pike rises; on the right is the long, quiet valley of Coledale, its Grisedale slopes defended by wiry heather and long fans of scree and therefore not recommended for descent.

Soon it is necessary to leave the Sleet How ridge, which becomes submerged in the pines of Hospital Plantation, to follow the very obvious track down past Lanty Well, conspicuously marked on the large-scale Ordnance Survey maps but in fact nothing more than a reed-fringed pool below a spring. Above a disused quarry the track makes a detour to avoid the marshy upper course of Masmill Beck, then sets a course down the broad ridge of **Kinn**, at a very easy gradient. It has been suggested that the German miners who came to the Keswick area in the sixteenth century named this substantial buttressing ridge (Kinn means 'chin' in German) and they may even have descended along it, at first easily but then steeply on the last section down to the road at the bottom of Whinlatter Pass.

The worst of this steep section can be avoided by following a zigzag keeping close to the edge of the plantation, north of the deeply eroded main track, but most pedestrians seem to prefer the unpleasant direct plunge down the badly worn trench. Both routes arrive at the road, and a right turn quickly brings you to the village of **Braithwaite**. This is a surprisingly large village, with a great deal of recent housing development. It was formerly one of the centres of the woollen industry (in common with other villages around Keswick) and provided the original site for the Cumberland Pencil Company, which was founded here in 1868 but moved to Keswick after a fire thirty years later.

Keswick is now an easy two-mile walk across the flood plains of Newlands Beck and the River Derwent, by any one of three routes. The most direct crosses Braithwaite Bridge and heads for Portinscale, but does suffer from the proximity of the vastly improved A66. Other possibilities are to go further north, to Bog House and across the drainage channels around Newlands Beck to How, then pleasantly along the bank of the River Derwent under the bypass to the suspension footbridge over the river, or to head south along lanes to Little Braithwaite and Ullock, then by footpath to Portinscale.

Neither of these two latter routes has a great deal to commend it at this stage of the walk, so leave Braithwaite along the Keswick road, cross the A66 with care and turn left along a stretch of the former road, now a rather forlorn-looking cul-de-sac, to cross the embanked Newlands Beck at Braithwaite Bridge. Immediately beyond the bridge take the path running along a field boundary between a rough track and the road, and curve round the little hump of Hodgson How to recross the A66 and join a lane on the outskirts of Portinscale. Bear right at the junction (the excellent Farmer's Arms is on the left) into the centre of the village. The way to Keswick (also followed by the fourth leg of the Lakeland Horseshoe, where full details can be found) passes The Tower Hotel, crosses the Derwent on the incongruous but functional suspension bridge and approaches Keswick and journey's end over the river meadows.

THE VALLEY ROUTE

This is a gentle walk from Eskdale to Patterdale through fell country which deliberately avoids summits and opts for easy gradients, but is nevertheless worthy of the closest consideration because of the exceptional views *of* rather than *from* the high peaks. Suitable for every type of walker, it emphasises the close relationship between mountain and dale which gives the Lake District its special appeal.

1 BURNMOOR
Boot to Wasdale Head (6 miles/10km)

This short but varied and delightful walk through superb scenery offers an excellent introduction to the fells of the western Lake District, especially as an afternoon stroll after a ride up lower Eskdale on the Ravenglass and Eskdale narrow-gauge railway, which has its terminus at Dalegarth station, close to the village of Boot. On the fellside above Dalegarth can be seen the disused workings of the Nab Gill iron ore mine, opened in the 1870s by the Whitehaven Mining Company and the main reason for the construction of the railway. Ore extracted at the mine was transported on the railway, which at that time had a 3ft gauge, to Ravenglass. The mine closed down in 1912 but the railway was acquired by the Keswick Granite Company, converted to its present 15in gauge, and pressed into service to export the pinkish red granite so characteristic of Eskdale.

Passengers were also carried during this second phase of the line's history, but this was not a commercial proposition and on several occasions the railway seemed doomed, most notably

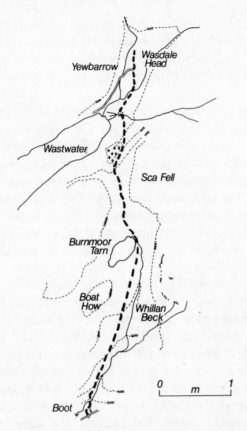

when the granite quarries were closed in 1953. In 1960, however, it was taken over by the trust which now runs it almost exclusively as a tourist attraction, with steam-hauled trains on most journeys and a choice of open or closed carriages to cater for Eskdale's rather fickle weather. During the height of the summer season there are as many as sixteen trains daily, though seven or eight is more typical of the summer as a whole.

The pleasant village of **Boot**, which lies slightly away from the main road up the valley, is comparatively unknown yet is full of interest. Down a lane to the south is St Catherine's Chapel, in a superb situation on the banks of the Esk, close to the route of the Roman Way. The lane north of the valley road leads between walls of pink Eskdale granite to a corn mill next to a fine packhorse bridge over the Whillan Beck. There was a mill operating in Boot from the thirteenth century onwards, and this one continued in operation until the 1920s; restoration began in 1975 and the fine drying loft above the waterwheel is now open to visitors.

The seventeenth-century packhorse bridge at the end of the village street is the starting point for the Valley Route, which begins by following the valley of the **Whillan Beck** for some two miles or so up to Burnmoor Tarn. Fork right two hundred yards above the bridge and climb quite steeply above a little wood, with the beck tumbling attractively over huge granite blocks in a series of miniature waterfalls. On the opposite bank is Gill Bank Farm, and above this stood what was the highest building in the valley, a carding mill which is now in a ruined condition.

The track rises steadily through the intake fields and then reaches the open fell, a rich and colourful landscape of heather, bracken and firm turf with the lower slopes of Scafell dominating the outlook across the beck to the north-east. The low, sprawling hill of **Boat How** fills the north-western horizon, and it is tempting to make the detour onto this little-visited fell to visit the stone circles and burial mounds which are liberally scattered around its higher slopes. Just beyond Boat How, though unsuspected from the path, is the secret valley of Miterdale, now almost unpopulated but previously the source of horrific stories concerning robberies and murder at one of the valley's farms. It is more practical, however, to stick to the path as it ascends gently past a couple of burial mounds and then the ruined dwelling on Eller How to reach the hollow containing Burnmoor Tarn.

This main track across the low, heather-covered pass of Burnmoor is known as the Old Corpse Road and was the route over which the dead were carried, their coffins strapped to a horse's back, from the hamlet of Wasdale Head to the chapel at Boot in the period before the tiny church at Wasdale Head was licensed for burials in the early nineteenth century. It is perhaps inevitable that legends abound of horses galloping off into the mist which

Burnmoor Tarn
and Yewbarrow

so often clothes the moor in winter, and Burnmoor is said to be haunted by at least one such horse still carrying its burden. The most entertaining story concerns the horse which, whilst carrying the mortal remains of a nagging wife, bumped the coffin into a tree and, much to the chagrin of the husband, thereby revived the old woman. When she died again the husband was at pains to ensure a peaceful journey for the coffin on its way to Boot.

Burnmoor Tarn is, indeed, a haunting place with, as Walt Unsworth has said, 'some indefinable quality . . . that makes it uniquely attractive' (others have suggested that it is desolate and dreary, but presumably they did not pause long enough to let the atmosphere seep in). It is one of the largest tarns and stands in a peaty waste, with only a glimpse of Yewbarrow as an appetiser for the full panorama of the fells around Wasdale Head, and yet it is full of character, some no doubt imparted by the darkly brooding Burnmoor Lodge, a particularly isolated hut which is still in use. Regrettably, **Scafell** turns its unappealing back on this scene and appears from here to be merely a large and formless fellside. The bilberry slopes of Illgill Head, away to the left, are much more appealing, as are the inquisitive donkeys which seem to congregate around the tarn.

Cross Whillan Beck near its outlet from the tarn and then, within a matter of yards, cross Hardrigg Gill, the main feeder. This oddity arises from the diversion by glacial action of Burnmoor Tarn's outflow, which can clearly be seen from the map to have previously been channelled in the direction of Miterdale. The path now rises very slowly across rather wet ground past Maiden Castle, twenty feet in diameter and probably used as a defensive earthwork, to the top of the pass at a mere 977ft. Now the view really opens out, with **Wastwater**, surely the most dramatic and awe inspiring of all the lakes, away to the left and the semi-circle of splendid peaks, seemingly springing out of the ground in the hamlet of Wasdale Head, dominating the scene in front and to the right. Across the main valley the deep trench of Mosedale below its surrounding fells is an unforgettable sight.

Start to descend from the col towards Wasdale on a broad path which gradually steepens and becomes loose and quite badly eroded in places by the side of Fence Wood, where the Green Howe route from Scafell (used by the Lakeland Horseshoe) joins from the right. Keep on above the wall past Brackenclose, cross Lingmell Gill, then turn right above Lizaholm Wood to keep on the east bank of Lingmell Beck, the main stream on the valley floor. Eventually, near Down in the Dale, cross the beck and meet the valley road near the open green and the former village school of **Wasdale Head**. The Wasdale Head Inn, which acts as the focus of the hamlet, is only about three hundred yards along the road.

The first settlers probably took on the unenviable task of taming the wild and stony valley head in the early years of the twelfth century, and it is likely that they began at Burnthwaite (literally 'the clearing among the borrans' or heaps of stones). Like Brotherilkeld in Eskdale, it is one of the earliest and greatest of the dalehead sheep farms, and indeed until comparatively recently it consisted of the two farms of High and Low Burnthwaite. By 1578 there were seventeen tenants at Wasdale Head, all of whom had a share in the arable and pasture land of

Wasdale Head field, the common field of the village. The boundaries of this common field, which covered about 345 acres, can still be traced in the stone-walled enclosures in the dale bottom. Each of the tenants was also entitled to use the common grazing land, which extended to around six thousand acres.

There is no formal record of the disappearance of the open field, although its demise was finally secured by the enclosure award granted in January 1808, and only the thick stone walls of the intake fields and occasional huge piles of stones painstakingly cleared from the pastures indicate its site. Some of these stone walls, uniquely substantial and intricate (some in places where there is no need for a wall, simply a need to get rid of the ubiquitous boulders), have suffered in the past few decades as the lanes have been widened to accommodate the motor car, and others have been neglected and in places have collapsed.

The remarkably small church, standing alone in its thicket of yews, dates from the early eighteenth century (though, as mentioned earlier, no burials were allowed here for another hundred years). With its tiny combined nave and chancel and equally small and simple bell-cote, it lays claim – along with several others – to the title of smallest church in the country. A panel in one window reads 'I will lift up mine eyes unto the hills from whence cometh my strength', a poignant reminder of the graves of eminent climbers in the churchyard outside.

The permanent population of the hamlet has never been more than forty or fifty, and this despite the growth of tourism, which came late to this isolated dalehead on the unfashionable western side of the Lake District but has now become an important factor in the local economy. The first to recognise the potential was Will Ritson, who was born at Row Foot in Wasdale Head in 1808. Ritson was a farmer and huntsman who, knowing the fells intimately, offered his services as a mountain guide as the first climbers began to arrive in the valley and then, as the influx grew, astutely obtained a licence for part of the farmhouse at Row Foot and renamed it The Huntsman Inn.

The reputation of the dale, its inn and its innkeeper spread rapidly and by the late nineteenth century Wasdale Head was

Scafell Pike and Scafell

Mecca for the new breed of mountaineers. 'Auld Will' Ritson was at the centre of it all, celebrated as a great sportsman and true wit as well as 'the world's greatest liar'. Ritson died at Nether Wasdale in 1890, having retired from the running of the inn a decade earlier. His memorial is the waterfall a few hundred yards away in Mosedale, now named Ritson Force. The inn was taken on by the Tysons, who rebuilt it in the 1880s (the original inn can still be seen as an annexe) and attempted to improve its image by calling it The Wastwater Hotel. Since then the name has varied from time to time but at present it is The Wasdale Head Inn, with an excellent, comfortable and recently renovated bar, Ritson's Bar, selling a range of real ale of which the old man himself might well have approved.

The inn lies at the centre of the hamlet, which consists of a handful of farmhouses at Row Head, Middle Row and Row Foot, the church across the fields, the former school and vicarage, and a scattering of farmsteads in the bottom of the valley. The one narrow road has its traffic problems in summer, for its capacity and that of the car parks at Wasdale Head is strictly limited, and these problems are also apparent on the day of the Wasdale Head Show, which takes place on the second Saturday in October. Sheepdog trials, displays of shepherds' crooks, fell racing, hound trails, Lakeland sports such as Cumberland wrestling and tug-of-war compete for attention in this successor to the original shepherds' meet.

Whatever the problems of Wasdale Head's huge popularity in high summer, it is always easy to escape from the crowds. The track past Burnthwaite across the lower slopes of Great Gable is usually pretty busy, but the variation up Gavel Neese (the next stage of the Valley Route) leads to quieter country, and the lane leading to the delightful packhorse bridge over Mosedale Beck at the rear of the inn is an excellent escape route. The single-arched bridge, probably dating from the eighteenth century, once supported the main road from Nether Wasdale (also known as Strands) to Wasdale Head when this ran along the west side of the beck instead of crossing it at Down in the Dale Bridge. Now it carries only the green track leading into the fine side-valley of Mosedale (part of the Lakeland Horseshoe route). And then there is **Yewbarrow** (2,058ft), frowning over the rear of the hotel, a superb whale-backed mountain with plenty of exposed rock and a panorama from the summit that has few equals. No wonder Wasdale Head is still Mecca for many Lake District enthusiasts!

2 MOSES' TROD AND HONISTER
Wasdale Head to Rosthwaite (9 miles/14km)

The most direct route between Wasdale and Borrowdale leads over Sty Head Pass to Seathwaite and Seatoller, but in summer especially this can prove to be a really tiresome walk along crowded and badly eroded tracks. In particular, the path across the lower slopes of Great Gable from Burnthwaite to Sty Head, deeply scored into the fellside, is in appalling condition and should be avoided at all costs. The alternative way described here admittedly does not seek out the lowest crossing or confine itself to valleys all the way, but it is quieter, uses an ingeniously

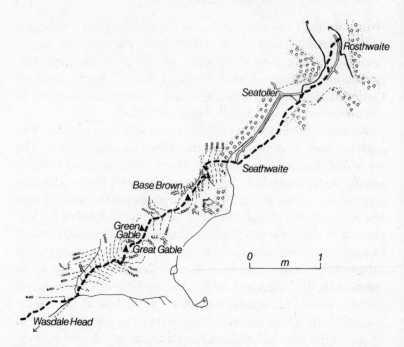

devised route and has tremendous views over the western fells
and dales.

The alternative route is known as Moses' Trod (or Moses'
Sledgate) and is reputed to have come into existence as a whisky
smuggler's route from Honister to Wasdale and the coastal
plain. Certainly it was in regular use in the early days of
quarrying at Honister Crag, when the slate was exported via
Wasdale on sledges. Now it is a well-known track skirting
round to the west of Great Gable and the ridge continuing
northwards to Grey Knotts, although until popularised by
Wainwright and others it was indistinct in places and in danger
of falling into disuse as a through route. Combined with a
descent of the old quarry road from Honister to Seatoller, it now
provides a superb walk amongst striking fells, yet except in the
initial ascent of the lower slopes of Gavel Neese, the steep south-
west ridge of Great Gable, it is nowhere difficult and in some
sections is exhilaratingly fast.

Take the lane running north-east from Wasdale Head and

skirt the farm buildings at Burnthwaite on their left; the craggy
Wasdale face of Great Gable dominates the scene ahead, with
Great End providing a suitably dour companion at the head of
the valley. After a quarter of a mile cross Gable Beck on a wide
modern footbridge and immediately turn left and begin to climb
on the firm turf which characterises the lower slopes of Gavel
Neese. Progress will probably be pitifully slow on this
unremittingly steep ridge, but there is compensation at each of
the inevitable resting places in the increasingly awesome
panorama of Wasdale, from the Scafell range to Wastwater,
backed by the Screes, and Yewbarrow.

At around mid-height on **Great Gable** (2,949ft) the character
of the ridge changes, unpleasantly loose scree replacing the grass
and heather. Ahead on the ridge can be seen the rocky outline of
the White Napes, a good scrambling route to the top of Great
Gable (see the Heart of Lakeland route for an account of this
ascent), with the prominent boulder known as Moses' Finger
jutting 8ft out of the scree some way below the crags. Fortunately, the route bears left a hundred feet below Moses' Finger
and crosses the scree above Gable Beck, gaining height much
more gently. The path can now be followed fairly easily to the
col at Beck Head.

Gavel Neese, Great Gable

Moses, so local legend has it, was a quarryman employed at Honister who found a profitable use for his spare time by making whisky from the bog water at a still on the slopes of Fleetwith Pike. His customers were the farmers of Wasdale, and he devised the route now known as Moses' Trod as a fast, level and above all secret way of crossing the fells behind Great Gable. Other legends have grown around the original story, and it is also claimed that Moses (or his successor) was involved with smugglers at Ravenglass and in stealing wadd, or graphite, from the mine on the other side of Grey Knotts. This last theory is more plausible than it appears at first sight as the graphite was so valuable that the mine was protected by armed guards.

Beck Head, the col separating Great Gable from Kirk Fell, lies at about 2,030ft, and although the approach along Moses' Trod, here only a narrow path overshadowed by the vast scree fans and shattered cliffs of the Gable, is an easy walk, the col itself is exposed and often very windy. The only real features of interest are the two tarns, the smaller one seasonal and therefore not really a true tarn. The larger one is only about thirty yards long and a good deal less across, but both have the distinction of being bisected by the fence posts of the former Ennerdale boundary fence, which pursues a straight line across the col.

Follow the fence posts east for a while (the right of way shown in green on the Ordnance Survey map is again, as in other places on the Lake District Outdoor Leisure maps, hopelessly inaccurate as a representation of what actually happens on the ground), then aim north-east into Stone Cove, a well-named repository of angular boulders which have fallen from the precipitous face of Gable Crag, a less well-known cliff than the Napes on the other, more accessible, side of Great Gable but equally impressive. High up the crag are the scanty remains of a stone hut attributed to Moses, and said to have been a store for his illegal whisky (and/or graphite). The highest place ever chosen for a building in England, it now has only a few foundation stones left, but is just about recognisable.

Moses' Trod now crosses the River Liza close to its source, with an excellent vista down the valley into the forests of

Ennerdale and the High Stile range

Ennerdale and across to the High Stile range and, nearer at hand, Haystacks. The path is now contouring the hillside below Green Gable, the insignificant northern twin of Great Gable, at around two thousand feet. Cross Tongue Beck near a sheepfold which can provide useful shelter, and continue roughly north across broken terrain between Brin Crag and Brandreth, with fine views north-west to the Ennerdale and Buttermere fells. The remains of the Ennerdale boundary fence are crossed again on the western slopes of Brandreth, and the path then continues below the summit of Grey Knotts to reach the forlorn remains of the Drum House, the winding gear shed at the summit of the course chosen for the former tramway running from Honister Pass to Dubs Quarry. Follow the old tramway steeply down to the top of the pass. As an alternative to the Drum House route, which can be wet underfoot in places, a path bearing right from the boundary fence can be picked up as far as the top of **Grey Knotts** (2,287ft), a fine viewpoint and one which is so easily reached that it really should be picked off.

The quarries at **Honister** would seem to have been in continuous production since at least 1643, and certainly there is firm evidence that they were already being worked on a large scale a century later. Ironically, the best quality green slate is situated at the top of Honister Crag, now much disfigured but still a prodigious piece of rock scenery. The result has been a succession of ingenious ways of getting the slate down from the crags. At first sledges or barrows crammed full of slate were manoeuvred down the side of the mountain at speed, either down the rock face or the screes, to Honister Pass. The slate was then taken along Moses' Trod over the high fells to Wasdale and the sea at Drigg near Ravenglass.

In the middle of the nineteenth century the route changed with the growth of the ports at Workington and Whitehaven, and the slate was now run down the screes to Gatesgarth and carted along Buttermere. But the most important change was achieved shortly after the Buttermere Slate Company took over the quarries in the 1870s, when the hazardous method of running the sledges down the scree was replaced by tramways running on inclined planes; the first of these Gravitational Railways was completed in 1881. More recently the tramways have fallen into disuse and the slate is brought down to the splitting sheds near the pass by lorries which reach the quarry face by an intricate zigzag route up the steep fellside.

The scars of past and present quarrying activity are all too obvious on the crags on both sides of Honister Pass, and it is unlikely that the passage of time will ever soften the impact. Honister has the misfortune to sit astride a zone of intensely deformed rocks, so that the slate is markedly fissile and splits evenly and cleanly to give easily workable flakes. Nevertheless, what is bad for the environment is good for the local economy, and even today quarrying is as important an employer as catering in the Lake District National Park, with one in ten of the workforce employed in the industry. The high-quality slate is very much in demand, though nowadays it is required as much for ornamental uses as for the more traditional purpose of roofing.

Leave Honister Pass on the busy tarmac road heading towards Seatoller and Borrowdale, but quickly bear left onto the old toll road, which runs just to the north of the present motor road almost all the way to Seatoller. The surface is in places pleasant and grassy, in others worn and uneven, but it forms an excellent alternative to the main road over the pass, which connects the popular tourist valleys of Borrowdale and Buttermere and is inevitably crowded in summer. Yet the old toll road could have been chosen for the main route over Honister Pass when this was surfaced for the first time in 1934; only the demand for £2,000, which was considered excessive, prompted the building of a new road on much steeper gradients. As a result the quarry road is now a quiet lane descending easily over the lower slopes of Dale Head to the hamlet of Seatoller.

Seatoller began life as a single farm occupied only during the summer (the Norse settlers called it 'the saetr', or summer dwelling, 'by the alder tree') and, although it expanded slightly in succeeding centuries, it remained a very small cluster of farm buildings under the rocky fells at the foot of Honister Pass until the expansion of the Honister quarries led to the building of quarrymen's cottages in the constricted valley of Hause Gill. Now the place has a distinctly split personality, with recent developments catering for tourists superimposed onto a previously isolated hamlet.

Take the footpath leading east out of Seatoller (before the lane from Seathwaite comes in from the right) and head towards Johnny Wood. The River Derwent is crossed here by Folly Bridge, a packhorse bridge but one which carries only a farm track; the form of the arch is circular on one side, elliptical on the other. The bridge was constructed in 1781 and cost £25. Just south is Mountain View, a block of eight houses built for quarry workers in the late nineteenth century. The path then enters Johnny Wood, a typical indigenous Lake District oak wood, protected as a Site of Special Scientific Interest. The Lake District Naturalists Trust, together with the National Trust, has laid out a nature trail through the wood.

The most interesting feature of Johnny Wood is its remarkable variety of ferns, mosses and liverworts, which thrive here because of the very high rainfall in upper Borrowdale. The tree cover is predominantly oak, but there are also patches of sycamore, the occasional larch, and typical Lakeland shrubs including mountain ash, hazel and holly. The wetter and poorer ground, unable to support oak, is mainly colonised by birch. Parts of the wood have survived for centuries with only occasional cutting for use in charcoal making. It is possible to make a fairly long detour across High Doat to inspect the waterfall at Scaleclose Force, but this cannot really be recommended. Instead, keep to the lower slopes to reach the bridge over the River Derwent at Longthwaite.

Across the river from Longthwaite is a particularly fine example of a terminal moraine, the glacial feature deposited at the edge of the ice as it slowly retreated up Borrowdale. A series of moraines can be picked out on the flat valley floor of the Derwent from the rock bar at The How, just south of Rosthwaite, to Burthwaite Bridge where Comb Gill enters the river. Opposite Longthwaite the river is gradually eroding the glacial material and exposing the sand, clay and assorted boulders of which it is composed. Except for the rocky knolls and ridges of moraine, the valley floor is notably flat and was the site of several glacial lakes; even today the whole area can be under water after heavy rain.

The cottages at Longthwaite, and across the river at Peathow, originally had external stone staircases, a typical feature of Lakeland domestic architecture, but with the addition of further rooms the staircases have been enclosed. Whilst the cottages have a timeless vernacular air about them, Longthwaite Bridge can be precisely dated to 1899, since it was built to replace one swept away in severe floods the previous year. From the bridge, walk south-east along the lane past Peathow to the main valley road, and turn left to reach the village of **Rosthwaite**, the focus of life in upper Borrowdale with its inns and village shop, and an excellent base for walking.

The village stands on the slopes of The How, a rocky intrusion into the Derwent flood plain, and has a number of pleasant stone cottages carefully sited just away from the main road. Nooka House, previously an inn and subsequently the village post office and shop, was well known for the card playing and dancing that went on there, but nowadays the village is quiet and respectable.

To the west are traces of the former open field in a series of small walled fields down in the valley, and beyond here is the New Bridge, another attractive packhorse bridge dating from the seventeenth century but oddly sited on a track leading nowhere. There are several short walks from the village suitable for an evening excursion, but none is better known than the trip across Grange Fell to Watendlath, an excellent, easy walk to round off a day spent in the midst of superb scenery.

3 ACROSS GREENUP EDGE
Rosthwaite to Grasmere (10 miles/16km)

The ancient route from Rosthwaite and Borrowdale across Greenup Edge to Grasmere heads first for the quiet valley of the Stonethwaite Beck, a classically U-shaped glaciated valley hemmed in beneath the forbidding cliffs of Bull Crag and Eagle Crag on the flanks of Glaramara, and Heron Crag and White Crag fronting the lower fells to the east. The hamlet of **Stonethwaite**, its whitewashed cottages clustered beneath the wooded slopes of Rosthwaite Fell, can be reached from Rosthwaite by road or, much better, by taking the lane heading to Hazel Bank, then turning sharp right immediately after crossing Stonethwaite Beck and keeping close to the stream for half a mile to Stonethwaite Bridge.

The greatest asset of Stonethwaite is its location away from the valley road, at the end of a narrow no-through-road. The peace of this delightful group of cottages in its sylvan setting is therefore assured, with rare exceptions, as when the valley was flooded to a depth of ten feet or more after the torrential rains of 13 and 14 August 1966, when over four inches of rain fell, turning the normally placid streams into fierce and destructive torrents. On the flat floor of the valley there are clues to the former location of the village's open field, as in Rosthwaite, but in Stonethwaite the old inn, with its serving hatch in the wall catering for travellers on the Greenup route, has been converted into cottages.

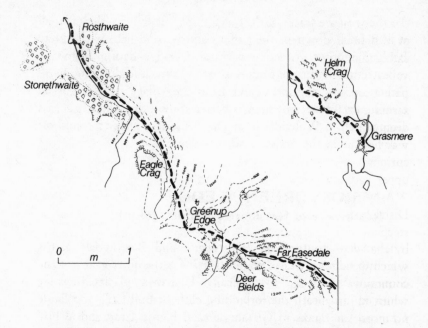

Take the lane signposted to Greenup Edge across Stonethwaite Bridge, go through a gate and turn right to follow a track keeping close to the beck below the thickly wooded fellside. The valley is pleasant if unremarkable, its most notable feature being the diminutive waterfall known as Galleny Force, but the way ahead is dominated by the breathtaking ramparts of **Eagle Crag**. The summit lies at a mere 1,650ft, but so majestic are the proportions of the crag, capping the wedge of high ground dividing the valley of Greenup Gill from the long and desolate bowl of Langstrath, that it fires the imagination in a way which many higher fells fail to do. At first sight, the layers of cliff overlooking the Greenup valley, with Eagle Crag itself above and in front of Pounsey Crag, seem quite unassailable, although there is an exciting scrambling route up the northern face of the fell.

At the confluence of Greenup Gill and Langstrath Beck, a place of tumbling, foaming waters and little rocky ravines, is Smithymire Island, unusually named and with an unusual history. It was to this island that the monks of Fountains Abbey brought their iron ore, won from the mine at Ore Gap on the 2,600ft

contour between Esk Pike and Bowfell. The island was the site
of a bloomery where the iron ore was smelted before being
carted along Borrowdale for distribution. Take the left-hand
valley, that of Greenup Gill, from the confluence and keep to the
path ascending gradually by the stream, with Eagle Crag high up
across the valley. The white waters of the cascades alternate with
deep, silent pools in the bed of Greenup Gill, but eventually the
way lies to the left of the main stream and also of Lining Crag, a
curious outcrop rising above the hummocky moraine of the
upper valley.

As **Greenup Edge**, on the central watershed of the Lake
District, is approached progress will be slowed not by the
steepness of the slope, which becomes gradually more gentle, but
by the wetness of the ground. Sadly the area around the col,
which separates the two fells – High Raise and Ullscarf – most
commonly quoted as the most central in the Lake District and
which might therefore be expected to be especially attractive, is
no more than a swamp. There is no foolproof way of avoiding
the worst of the marsh, although a detour to the south can sometimes prove useful.

The Stonethwaite Valley.

On the top of Greenup Edge is a guidepost near the remains of a fence. Paths to Ullscarf and High Raise force their way through marshy ground to north and south respectively. The priority now is to identify correctly the path leading down to Far Easedale, and to keep to it for the next half mile to the head of that valley, avoiding the temptation to veer left into the isolated and exceptionally wet wasteland of the Wythburn valley. The path cuts across several of the headwaters of the Wyth Burn, but keeps generally just south of east (a path to Thirlmere will be seen heading north-east) and rises to the col separating Wythburn and Far Easedale, which is indicated by a second line of fence posts.

The head of Far Easedale is a good place to reflect on the remarkably varied scenery encountered in following the ancient trade route between Borrowdale and Grasmere. The valleys of Stonethwaite and Far Easedale could hardly be more different. The former is gentle and well wooded, with a rippling stream and a flat flood plain; even the crags, partly masked by the trees, appear picturesque rather than savage. Far Easedale, on the other hand, is walled by fierce crags reaching up almost to the skyline from the rocky ravine of the beck in its upper reaches. The slopes are strewn with boulders of all descriptions and the overall effect is of a rough, untamed landscape far removed from the sylvan peacefulness on the other side of Greenup Edge.

Nevertheless, scenically **Far Easedale** rates very highly, its crags and their individual features soon becoming imprinted on the memory. First, however, the steep slopes down into the head of the valley have to be negotiated, on a path which keeps close to the stream to avoid the worst of Moor Moss. To the right is the broad front of Ferngill Crag, and up on the left is the summit ridge of Calf Crag, with the attractive rocky bastion known as Pike of Carrs lower down the fellside. The path crosses Far Easedale Gill just above an attractive waterfall (there is no real path beyond this point on the northern bank of the gill, although the map shows a right of way), then follows the stream as it foams down a series of rocky steps below the gaunt grey cliff of Deer Bield Crag.

Well known to rock climbers as the location of several particularly exacting rock climbs, **Deer Bields** is a magnificent and notably steep crag with a detached central buttress. The ascent of the buttress is technically labelled as 'extremely severe' and includes strenuous climbing on overhanging rock in very exposed positions. Down below, the Valley Route follows the rather less exacting path along Far Easedale Gill and recrosses it on Stythwaite Steps, an easy succession of stepping stones across the shallow stream. Stythwaite, 'the thwaite of the stee', refers to a clearing in the valley of the stee, or ladder, and has the same meaning as in Sty Head, where the ladder is the steep climb up to the pass. The lower section of Far Easedale was in fact previously referred to as Stythwaite.

The fell to the left at this point is Gibson Knott, and the cliff overlooking the valley is Horn Crag, its fine buttress an excellent landscape feature but too broken up by vegetation to attract the climbing fraternity. In the recesses on the steep face of the crag a few junipers have gained a toe-hold and cling tenaciously to the rock. The next section of the old packhorse route is enlivened only by its bridges. First is the simple but effective Willy Goodwaller Bridge, of packhorse type but used only for driving sheep to and from the higher pastures. A little further downstream is New Bridge, its predecessor destroyed in the floods of 1963.

By now the twin valley of Easedale has joined from the right, its Sour Milk Gill dropping over waterfalls as it makes its way from Easedale Tarn down to the level of the main stream, now known simply as Easedale Beck. While the fellside away to the right is shapeless and undistinguished, the path is now traversing the slopes of **Helm Crag**, its summit hidden up on the left but well seen in retrospect later in the walk. Helm Crag is one of the most memorable fells in the Lake District, although its summit is one of the lowest at 1,299ft. The highest point can only be attained by an enjoyable piece of rock scrambling, and the summit rocks are well known to travellers on the main road between Keswick and Ambleside, the most conspicuous of them having been labelled 'The Lion and the Lamb' and 'The Old

Woman Playing the Organ' because of their startling appearance from various viewpoints. Undoubtedly a detour to the top of the fell (turning left away from the Valley Route at Kitty Crag) or an evening expedition would be time well spent.

At the junction of lanes and paths at Kitty Crag, just below Easedale House, take the lane running parallel to Easedale Beck and follow it as it curves round to Goody Bridge, on which the beck is crossed. Continue along the lane, with the National Trust property at Butharlyp Howe – its wooded knolls a delightful foreground for views up to Dunmail Raise and the western side of the Helvellyn range – on the left, and enter the large village of Grasmere through an attractive parkland landscape.

It is difficult for anyone who has experienced it in the height of summer to remain objective about the village of **Grasmere**. The lake, some distance away to the south, remains hauntingly beautiful. The Wordsworth connection, in the Town End part of the settlement near the lake, has been handled reasonably discreetly in view of the phenomenal number of visitors it attracts. But the village itself is a drab, mostly modern place with a glossy veneer of commercialism masking its true lack of interest. There is little doubt here that the main aim is to separate the tourist from his money, and it is one which is achieved unashamedly and with a total lack of subtlety.

Slightly away from all this vulgarity is the parish church of St Oswald, much visited by admirers of Wordsworth but worth a close look in its own right for its features of architectural interest. The exterior is thickly coated with pebbledash, but the nave and tower probably date from the fourteenth century. Inside the plan is unusual and highly interesting. A wall, which does not touch the ridge of the roof, divides the interior longitudinally, and below the wall there is a separate roof for each arcade. These roofs appear to have been constructed in the seventeenth century. In a corner of the churchyard close to the river are the Wordsworth graves, on a site chosen by the poet near the eight yew trees which he planted.

The church is the scene each year, during the weekend closest

to St Oswald's Day (5 August), of the most famous of the rushbearing ceremonies. The origins of the practice are straightforward. Until about 1840 the church had an earthen floor, and
so rushes were strewn thickly each autumn to cover the dank and
damp surface. Ceremonies evolved out of this simple necessity –
in much the same way as well-dressing in the Peak District – and
the present-day occasions in Grasmere and Ambleside are the
survivors of many similar rituals, although they have inevitably
been embellished over the years for the benefit of visitors.

The other big event in Grasmere's calendar is the biggest and
best of all sports meetings in the Lake District, held on the
Thursday closest to 20 August. Enormous crowds are attracted
in good weather to the tremendous natural amphitheatre in
which the sports are held, a bowl-shaped ground surrounded by
craggy fells. The sports include hound trailing, pole jumping,
athletics, Cumberland freestyle wrestling and the exciting and
extremely competitive Guides Race, one of the most famous of
all the fell races.

The fabric of the village, apart from the church, is largely
modern and of no great interest, and the few older buildings
which remain have generally been altered. One of the more well
known is the former school, now the shop selling the speciality
of the village, Sarah Nelson's Grasmere gingerbread. Even better
known, though some distance away from the village centre, is
Dove Cottage, the home of William Wordsworth from 1799 to
1808. The tiny cottage, probably seventeenth century and
certainly typical of the period, is open to the public. The small
museum in a former barn across the lane has some of the poet's
manuscripts and other memorabilia. A more attractive destination for a short excursion, however, would be the rocky summit
of Helm Crag, by the route already indicated.

4   THE HELVELLYN RANGE AND GRISEDALE
Grasmere to Patterdale (10 miles/16km)

This final section of the Valley Route uses the much-trodden path across Grisedale Hause, but the outstanding mountain scenery and wealth of interest in the valleys more than make up for the crowds which could be encountered. For those determined to avoid such popular and, unfortunately, eroded tracks there is a longer and much quieter alternative using the little-known Scandale Pass. However, it is considerably further and its route, below Nab Scar to Rydal and Low Sweden Bridge, and then north along Scandale and over the pass to Brothers Water and Patterdale, is rather less interesting.

Start the final leg of the Valley Route by retracing the previous day's route as far as Goody Bridge, then bear right along the lane to Underhelm – the summit rocks of Helm Crag are prominent on the left – and cross the River Rothay on Low Mill Bridge. The lane leads to the main A591 Keswick to Ambleside road just to the north of The Travellers Rest Inn. This road, the most important through route in the Lake District and the only one which succeeds in crossing the main east–west watershed, follows a zone of weakened rock which has been worn down to give a series of valleys and low cols running from Windermere to Dunmail Raise, Thirlmere and the Glenderaterra valley. Close to the highest point of the route, Dunmail Raise is a round cairn which is said to commemorate Dunmail, last king of the Cumbrians. The old road passed close to the cairn, east of the present road, which came into being after a turnpike trust was set up in 1761 to improve the route between Kendal and Cockermouth.

Cross the main road and begin to ascend by the side of Tongue Gill, attractively at first with a little wood shielding the stream from view and Tonguegill Force, heard rather than seen because of the problems in approaching it, down in the ravine to the right. On the open fellside there is nothing of great moment in the immediate scene and it becomes rather a slog, with Grisedale

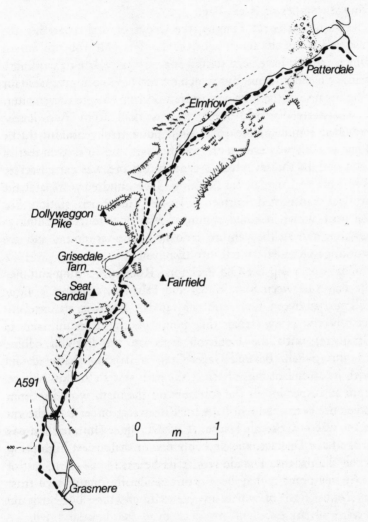

Patterdale

Elmhow

Dollywaggon
Pike

Grisedale
Tarn

Seat
Sandal ▲

▲ Fairfield

A591

0   m   1

Grasmere

Hause seemingly very little nearer across the broad shoulder of
Seat Sandal. There is a choice of routes where Little Tongue Gill
joins from the left, and indeed the wider of the two paths heads
up the tributary valley. However, keep right along Tongue Gill
itself, for this path, which is slightly indistinct at first but soon
improves, is shorter and follows a better line, although it can be

damp where it fords the many rivulets which run into the stream from the slopes of Great Rigg.

High up on Great Tongue, the wedge of land separating the two becks, are the remains of the Tongue Gill iron ore mines, which seem to have been started at a very early date to work rich veins of haematite ore, but which cannot have been profitable for long because of the high cost of transporting the ore to a smelter. The easterly Fairfield mine was worked from two levels; Providence mine, close to the old pony track climbing Little Tongue Gill, was even more prolific, with up to sixteen feet of solid ore. In the seventeenth century the ore was carted across Red Bank to Langdale for smelting. Two hundred years later the ore was transported fourteen miles to Windermere station, but the price which it could command was only fourteen shillings per ton, and so the venture soon became uneconomic and the workings were left to fall into disrepair.

Continue along the Old Packhorse Road on its long climb to the hause between Seat Sandal and Fairfield, crossing Tongue Gill just above a fine series of rapids. There is an excellent retrospective view from this point of the tranquil lake of Grasmere, with the Coniston Fells on the horizon behind Loughrigg Fell. Beyond Gavel Crag, a striking shattered cliff with its attendant fans of scree, the path skirts a hollow which, from an inspection of the contours on the map, would seem to have once contained a tarn. A final steep section leads to the gap in the wall at Grisedale Hause, at 1,929ft the seventh highest pass in the Lake District, and probably one of the busiest high passes when the packhorse trade was at its height.

At this point it may be worth considering one of two short diversions, both of which involve extra climbing but bring the reward of an excellent prospect over the Lakeland fells. A straightforward ascent of 500ft close to the line of the wall on the left leads to the summit of **Seat Sandal** (2,415ft), generally regarded merely as a huge, grassy and uninteresting fell but with a fine panorama westwards from its summit cairn. Especially impressive is the mountain skyline from the serrated ridge of Crinkle Crags round to the conical Bowfell, Great End and

Pillar. The second possibility is to turn right at the hause and climb to the top of **Fairfield** (2,863ft), a fine mountain in its own right and the centre of a miniature mountain system with high ridges separated by deep coves which, at least to the north and east, are defiantly wild and craggy.

The Valley Route itself ignores these two opportunities to reach the heights, and having ascended Grisedale Hause is content to descend to **Grisedale Tarn**, which is in full view from the hause. The tarn, set on a ledge right at the head of Grisedale, is one of the most exposed in the Lake District, and its surface is often dark and windswept. The surrounding mountain scenery more than does justice to the tarn, however, with fiercely brooding crags and the bare slopes of high mountains reflected in its waters. One of the largest tarns in the area, Grisedale Tarn's rocky floor drops steeply to its maximum depth of 115ft, adding to the sense of drama in this bouldery, untamed hollow.

Go round the tarn, keeping to the path on its south-eastern shores, to the junction of routes just below its outlet. Uphill to the left lies the broad, scarred track zigzagging up the slopes of **Dollywaggon Pike** (2,810ft) on its way to Nethermost Pike and ultimately Helvellyn, one of the four Lakeland Three-thousanders and a place of pilgrimage for many tourists. The Old Packhorse Road from Grasmere is probably the most popular route to the summit, and hence can become very busy in the height of the season. Close to this path lies the Brothers Rock, inscribed at the behest of Canon Rawnsley, vicar of Great Crosthwaite and a co-founder of the National Trust. The stone commemorates the last meeting of William Wordsworth with his brother John in 1800, five years before John's ship sank with no survivors.

The Valley Route takes the track heading downhill and to the right at the junction below the tarn, and proceeds down Grise-dale in the midst of tremendous rock scenery, particularly on the bold south-east face of Dollywaggon Pike to the left. The gullies scoring Tarn Crag and the cliffs of Falcon Crag are especially attractive, and to their right is the lip of the hanging valley of

Cock Cove. Across the valley is the long line of broken cliffs forming the Grisedale face of St Sunday Crag, an under-rated fell with a superb but very difficult scrambling route along Pinnacle Ridge to its summit.

Beyond Spout Crag the track passes Ruthwaite Lodge, built in 1854 as a shooting lodge, later used as a shelter for passengers on pony excursions from Patterdale to Helvellyn, but for a good many years now used as a climbing hut. The path curves right to follow the south bank of Ruthwaite Beck, an attractive stream with a series of small waterfalls and rapids and, just upstream from the lodge, two caves of uncertain age but probably man-made origin in its south bank. Above is the bouldery hollow of Ruthwaite Cove and, even higher up below the top crags of Nethermost Pike, Hard Tarn, a superb but little-visited high-level tarn in magnificent surroundings.

Some distance below Ruthwaite Lodge a choice has to be made between two different routes. A path branches off left across the beck and keeps to the northern side of Grisedale, eventually meeting the track across Birkhouse Moor from Helvellyn at Browend Plantation. The more direct (and more pleasant) route continues down to Grisedale Beck, crosses it on a simple bridge and remains on the south side of the valley, travelling along the lower slopes of St Sunday Crag.

Both paths have a fine view of Eagle Crag, the prominent buttress low down on the eastern approaches to Nethermost Pike, and the site of an ancient mine worked sporadically until the nineteenth century. It can hardly have been a financially rewarding venture, however, for there were usually only three or four miners at work there, and it now exists as a barely visible memorial to past enterprise. Beyond Eagle Crag is the fine hanging valley of Nethermost Cove, and on the skyline is the jagged outline of Striding Edge, the superb arête leading eastwards from Helvellyn and, despite its apparent difficulty as a walker's route, the most popular of the eastern approaches to the mountain.

The upper valley is marked on maps as Grisedale Forest, but there is little evidence on the ground to support the use of the

Elmhow Bridge, Grisedale

term. Crossing Plantation, a mixed coniferous and deciduous wood, is the highest woodland now existing. The path skirts the wood, leaving it close to a hogg-house (a rough winter shelter for yearling sheep), and continues to descend gradually and easily to reach the farm at **Elmhow**. Another very pleasant wood, planted with a mixture of hardwoods and larch and with a leavening of wild cherries, acts as a windbreak protecting the low, clustered farm buildings from the prevailing south-westerly winds.

The farm is linked to the Braesteads track and the main road by Elmhow Bridge, a classically simple seventeenth-century packhorse bridge. Instead of crossing the bridge, however, keep to the track following the south bank of Grisedale Beck closely and make for the farm of Thornhow, which lies on the lower slopes of the unromantic-sounding Birks. For once this initial impression is right since, except for the wall of rock facing Grisedale, the fell of Birks has very little to offer, except for a good prospect over Ullswater from the ridge running north-east of the summit. Beyond Thornhow the well-wooded parkland landscape of Glemara Park on the right forms a pleasant contrast to the lowland pastures and rough grazing of the Grisedale farms.

The path has now become a surfaced road, which is followed as far as the lane leading to Home Farm. Here there are two possibilities. The first is to keep to the road until it joins the main valley road at Grisedale Bridge, and then to turn right past the church and school building to reach the hotels and shops in the small village of **Patterdale** (which is also the destination of one of the legs of the Lakeland Horseshoe and is described there). The second possibility is to take the track heading south-east, in the angle between the surfaced road and the Home Farm lane, and cut across the shoulder of the hill to enter Patterdale just south of the hotels.

If time permits (and particularly if real ale is desired since when last surveyed there was none in Patterdale), the main road can be followed north to the tip of Ullswater and, with a diversion to the pier which accommodates the steamers which run the length of the lake to Pooley Bridge, to the village of Glenridding. The bar of The Glenridding Hotel is the place for real draught beer, but the highlight here is the superb setting of the fells around the head of Ullswater, preferably with the upper reaches of the lake itself shimmering in the late afternoon sun, an appropriately relaxing finish to the Valley Route.

THE HIDDEN VALLEYS

Kentmere–Harter Fell–Kentmere (15 miles/24km)

This long but comparatively easy walk starts from Kentmere Church, crosses into the still almost undiscovered valley of Longsleddale, and then takes the line of fells forming its eastern boundary to reach Gatescarth Pass and the shores of Haweswater. It then continues up Rough Crag and Long Stile, which can justifiably be regarded as the outstanding way to the top of High Street, before turning south-east across the plateau to Mardale Ill Bell, Harter Fell and the broad ridge declining to Shipman Knotts and, eventually, the path back to the village of Kentmere.

The approach to Kentmere, along the narrow road following the valley of the Kent upstream from Staveley, is one of delightful contrasts between the sylvan beauty near at hand and the rugged fells forming a backcloth at the head of the valley. About a mile south of the village is the former site of the Kent Mere, now part of one of the Lake District's most unlikely industries. The former lake occupied the flat valley floor opposite Millrigg and was about a mile long, but its natural dam of glacial moraine was breached towards the end of the nineteenth century and the lake was later completely drained. However, deposits of diatomaceous clay were discovered in the lake bed, and these are now dredged from the valley floor (creating a new artificial lake) and processed in a factory almost hidden in the trees.

Kentmere village lies almost at the end of the valley road, its farmhouses and cottages scattered on the slopes of the steeply incised River Kent. The church, with its dour grey, ashlar-faced west tower, has a sixteenth-century roof but the remainder dates

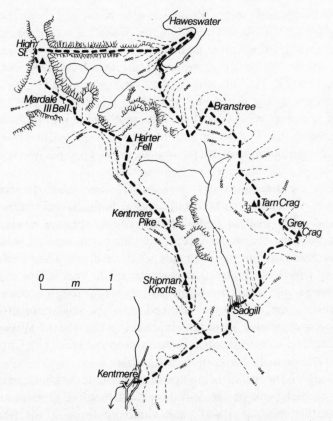

from the restorations of 1866 and 1950. Kentmere Hall, a private house west of the village, consists of a fourteenth-century pele tower with a rather later farmhouse attached to it, and was the birthplace in 1517 of the reformer Bernard Gilpin. Near the bridge over the river stood The Low Bridge Inn (now a private house), notorious as the first pub in England to lose its licence through drunkenness and immorality. Late drinking sessions for the navvies building Kentmere Reservoir in the nineteenth century led to complaints that the men were unfit for work and had taken to sleeping in the church porch; the landlord was finally brought before the magistrates at Kendal and stripped of his licence.

The walk starts from the church, descends the steep hill to

Low Bridge and crosses the fast-flowing Kent, and then follows the lane on the left to Green Quarter. Take the walled lane as it rises through the hamlet and onto the open fellside, eventually joining the packhorse route across the fells from Stile End to Longsleddale. The col, which follows the same band of Coniston Limestone as the Garburn Pass west of Kentmere, shows some evidence of ice erosion, and the limestone can be seen in some of the field walls. The flat summit of the pass is often rather boggy, but the going improves on the way down past Sadgill Wood into the long, unspoilt valley of Longsleddale.

The eighteenth-century packhorse bridge over the River Sprint, just below the farm buildings at **Sadgill**, marks the end of the valley road in Longsleddale. The bridge, the cluster of dwellings and the wooded slopes culminating in the dark wall of Goat Scar combine to form one of those classic Lake District views which encapsulate the character of the area in one scene. Above Sadgill, where the Sprint cuts its way through a rock bar, there is a narrow alluvial flat and then the wild head of the valley, culminating in rough slopes above the disused Wrengill Quarry and its ruined cottages, and a steep and rocky climb up to the Gatescarth Pass and over to Mardale.

Walk up the track leading upstream from the packhorse bridge on the east bank of the Sprint, but after only 200 yards turn right, just beyond a wall, and climb up through the intake towards the spine of Great Howe. Down to the right is Stockdale Farm, with an old lime kiln in the yard testifying to the presence of more Coniston Limestone. There is also a fine prospect southwards of the narrow trench of Longsleddale. Turn left to ascend the ridge, and pass a structure described as a cairn on the Ordnance Survey map, but actually a disused survey post used during the construction of the aqueduct carrying water from Haweswater reservoir towards Manchester. The rock outcrops of the lower part of the ridge give way to tough grass and occasional peat bogs on the way to **Grey Crag** (2,093ft), the first of eight summits to be scaled during the walk.

There is very little to say about the summit of Grey Crag, which is a pity because this is the most easterly of the 2,000ft summits in the Lake District and it marks the abrupt end of the high fells and the start of rolling moorland country more reminiscent of the Pennines. Certainly it is not on the itinerary of the vast majority of walkers, and those who do come here will probably press on quickly north-west towards Greycrag Tarn. It is worth keeping well to the right of the 'tarn' (which is reputedly haunted) because it seems to have seeped into the surrounding black, peaty mire, and its shallow basin is now only marked by an outbreak of rushes in the middle of the marsh.

Once the bogs and peat hags have been safely negotiated, there is only a very gentle slope to be climbed to reach **Tarn Crag** (2,176ft). The summit is marked by a small cairn, but a more imposing object is the remains of another survey post, a solid 15ft structure above the craggy western face of the fell. Buck-barrow Crag, a tremendous cliff crowding in on the track up the valley from Sadgill, is much the best feature of the mountain but is sadly well away from the route, which now continues on gentle slopes down to the marshy col at the head of Mosedale, an utterly desolate and remote valley in the Shap Fells. There follows a steady and rather dull climb alongside the wall up Selside Brow to the top of **Branstree** (2,333ft). Branstree has had a bad press, and it is easy to see why: the summit plateau is wide and devoid of interest, although the detour to the fine cairn above Artlecrag Pike has its rewards in a good view of Haweswater and the fells around Mardale Head.

Follow the fence south-west from Branstree down a steep grassy slope to Gatescarth Pass, and then turn right to follow the old packhorse route – formerly an important link between Longsleddale and Mardale, but much less so after the flooding of the latter valley and the hamlet of Mardale Green to create a much enlarged **Haweswater** – down alongside the remarkably straight ravine of Gatescarth Beck to the head of the reservoir.

In the early twentieth century Mardale Green was described by Bradley as 'a hamlet unforgettable for the charm of its romantic beauty and seclusion from the world'. The attractions included the ancient church, surrounded by yews, and the seventeenth-century Dun Bull, a low-ceilinged, many-roomed inn which hosted the shepherds' meet each November, with sheepdog trials, hound trailing, a hunt and a good deal of drinking over a period of some five or six days. All this ended with the acceptance of Manchester's proposal to raise the level of Haweswater by 95ft, doubling its length to six miles and drowning the valley, the ten-acre former common field and the village. Despite opposition, the reservoir and aqueduct came into operation in October 1941.

The effect on the landscape was dramatic, and even after four decades the scars have not healed. The problem lies in the appallingly ugly bleached shoreline which is exposed whenever the reservoir is drawn down. The shoreline has been described as 'obscene' and 'revolting', and certainly it is an alien intrusion into the impressive and natural fell country around the dalehead. Worse still, there is no life in the valley, since the new hotel is too far away from the dalehead and the new footpath skirting the north-west shore is too remote from the main centres and the best scenery to attract more than a handful of walkers.

Keep to the path skirting the north-west shore of Haweswater for almost half a mile, however, then double back along the crest of the ridge heading almost due west towards the High Street plateau. Accompanied by a wall, continue above Heron Crag and Eagle Crag and ascend the rocky ridge of Rough Crag, a magnificent route on rock, grass and occasionally peat. Eventually the slope eases and the slight depression of Caspel Gate, with its tiny tarn, comes into view. To the right is the vast glaciated hollow of Riggindale, empty except for the ruins of Riggindale Farm near the lake shore, whilst to the left is the giant and almost circular corrie tarn of Blea Water, backed magnificently by sheer rock walls rising a thousand feet above the tarn.

With a depth of over two hundred feet, Blea Water is deeper than any other Lakeland tarn (only Wastwater and Windermere among the fully fledged lakes are deeper). The moraine which dams the tarn is no more than eighty feet deep, testimony to the extent to which ice gouged out an over-deepened hollow beneath the sheer back wall of the corrie. Below the tarn is a further moraine which acted as a dam for a second tarn, but the barrier has long since been breached and only a few patches of moss and rushes remain to indicate its former location.

Beyond Caspel Gate the superb narrow, rocky arête known as Long Stile provides a direct and exhilarating way to the top of **High Street** (2,718ft), already described in some detail in the Lakeland Horseshoe and also visited during the course of the Roman Way walk. From the cairn at the top of Long Stile the summit, with its triangulation pillar, lies south-west across a wide plateau, and a more scenic route cuts across the peat hags above Blea Water Crag to the path leading to the fine summit cairn of **Mardale Ill Bell** (2,496ft). The views back to High Street and Long Stile, across the dark calm of Blea Water, are especially impressive (and notably so if the ridge leading down to Piot Crag is descended for some distance), and to the south the Ill Bell ridge is a prominent feature.

Cut above the fellside from the ridge above Piot Crag, keeping below the standard and relatively well-trodden path down to the Nan Bield Pass. This route is over rough ground but has the advantage of arriving almost directly above Small Water, an exquisite tarn in an absorbing setting between Mardale Ill Bell and Harter Fell, with the Nan Bield track leading the eye down the valley to Haweswater and beyond towards Penrith. It is then possible to contour around the fellside to reach the Nan Bield Pass, the highest point on the steep route between Mardale and Kentmere, and a true rocky pass between two pronounced spurs. On the Mardale side of the pass, above Small Water, are three remarkable little shelters, so small that they can only be entered on hands and knees.

The zigzags of the Nan Bield Pass can be followed down to Kentmere if the last real climb of the day looks too trying, but the ascent of the north-west ridge of Harter Fell, which rises from Nan Bield in a succession of steep and stony steps above Small Water Crag and the gully called Black John Hole, is well worth making. The flat top of **Harter Fell** (2,539ft) is a disappointment after this, although the view is extensive and is particularly good from the edge of the plateau, with Small Water

Blea Water and Long Stile

and Blea Water backed by the massive length and breadth of the High Street range.

The way south along the descending ridge from Harter Fell is decidedly timid after the excitement of the fells at the head of Mardale. A fence, which later becomes a wall, shows the way down The Knowe to a peaty depression and then over Brown Howe. The remarkable gash of Drygrove Gill, a ravine which may be a landslip, is the only item of interest, and this is situated some way down the Kentmere slopes of the fell. Kentmere Reservoir, built to regulate the flow of the river for the mills much further downstream, is seen particularly well from Brown Howe. The ridge here is flat, broad and grassy as it heads towards **Kentmere Pike** (2,397ft), generally an unprepossessing mountain with an equally dull summit, although the rocky eastern slopes of the fell are of a different character, with Raven Crag and Goat Scar presenting a ferocious face to the upper valley of the River Sprint.

South from the Ordnance Survey column on Kentmere Pike the walk continues across windswept moorland country, although after leaving the cairn overlooking the fine crags of Goat Scar there is a surprising change in scenery in the form of the rock outcrops which crown the summit of **Shipman Knotts** (1,926ft), a modest but remarkably rough-textured fell. Beyond the summit, the ridge begins to descend quite abruptly to the pass between Kentmere and Longsleddale which was used earlier in the walk. The extensive panorama ahead is dominated by the extremely broad and notably featureless plateau separating the two valleys, with only the lonely tarn of Skeggles Water providing a focus of attention. Turn right at the col and take the path down to Green Quarter and the village of Kentmere to complete a long, varied and fascinating walk on the still relatively unknown yet exceptionally interesting eastern fringes of the Lake District.

THE HEART OF LAKELAND

This three-day excursion, starting and finishing in Great Langdale, is a thrilling high-level introduction to some of the most spectacular peaks in the Lake District. The first day features Crinkle Crags and the exhilarating walk from Bowfell to Great End. The highlight of the second day's walk is the ascent of the magical mountain of Great Gable, while on the third day there are visits to the outstanding viewpoint of Glaramara and to the Langdale Pikes, and the extraordinary descent of Jack's Rake on Pavey Ark to Stickle Tarn and Great Langdale.

1   CRINKLE CRAGS AND BOWFELL
Great Langdale to Wasdale Head (12 miles/19km)

Start the walk from **The Old Dungeon Ghyll Hotel**, formerly a statesman farm on the sheltered south-facing slopes of the valley but now a superbly situated hotel with a rather basic public bar, the kind where deposits are levied to reduce the impact of over-exuberant climbers on the stock of beer glasses and the furnishings are decidedly spartan. The hotel, affectionately known as the ODG, has the added distinction of being the terminus for a surprisingly good bus route from Ambleside. On reaching the main valley road turn right, then sharply left instead of straight on to Stool End Farm and the start of the popular but worn-out path up The Band to Bowfell. Now head past a camp site and climb, still on the metalled road, past Wall End Farm.

Wall End, which like its neighbours is now owned by the National Trust, has a fine example of a late medieval drystone barn, constructed of carefully chosen boulders separated by layers

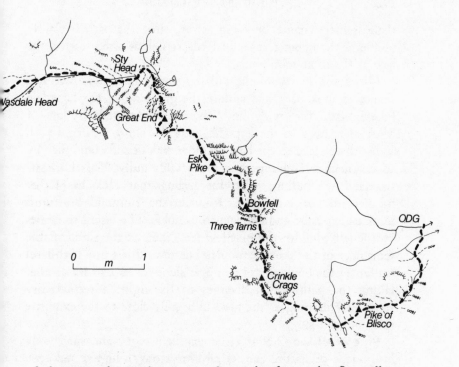

of slate. As the road steepens above the farm, the flat valley bottom of Great Langdale becomes even more pronounced, as does the evidence of glacial drift deposited along the side of the dale from Wall End along the flank of Side Pike. The flat floor was the site of a lake during the Ice Age, and was ponded back behind a rock bar at Chapel Stile. Even today the valley bottom can be turned into a shallow lake after an exceptionally heavy downpour, despite considerable efforts to control the flow of the becks from the two converging valleys of Mickleden and Oxendale.

To the right of the road, which leads over a low col to Blea Tarn and Little Langdale, is the rocky bed of Redacre Gill. Soon after the road diverges from the gill, take the footpath on the right and keep close to, but some way above, the stream, crossing a little rivulet and then the gill itself. The path follows the bank of the stream under the broken ramparts of Kettle Crag to its source on the higher slopes of Pike of Blisco. These days there is little chance of going astray, since the path is plainly visible in the upper reaches of Redacre Gill as a red scar on the face of the mountain.

Above the source of the gill the slope eases, and there is a chance to look back and admire the grouping of the Langdale Pikes, with the wide and obviously glaciated trough of Mickleden away to the left. The way lies along a cairned path across the plateau to the base of a low wall of cliffs, and then by an excellent scrambling route up a wide gully. This is classic Lakeland scrambling, with the feeling that rock has to be handled to make progress towards the summit, but with minimal exposure and very generous holds. The easiest route lies on the left edge for the first few feet, then on the right for the remainder of the short scramble. The reward is a fine high-level walk over the boulder-strewn upper slopes of Pike of Blisco and, taking the path which diverges to the right, a second easy scramble emerging at the head of a gully close to the exquisite little summit ridge.

Pike of Blisco (2,304ft) is an excellent mountain, spoilt only by its lack of stature and its position close to higher and even more magnificent fells. The summit lives up to its reputation, with rock outcrops in profusion and an excellent view from the highest point, which is crowned by a solidly built and dignified cairn. Even this cairn is, however, a shadow of its vandalised predecessor, a tall and distinctive pillar which was unmistakable even from the floor of Great Langdale 2,000ft below. From the slightly lower southern crags, the arc of the Coniston Fells can be seen across Wrynose Pass, while the summit rocks have the better view of Crinkle Crags, the pyramid of Bowfell and the trough of Great Langdale. From either outcrop the path down towards Red Tarn is easily made out.

This path descends steeply and stonily down the western side of Pike of Blisco, reaching a band of vividly red earth just before the col. The stream draining Red Tarn – a shallow and reed-fringed pool, suffering like all ridge tarns (except Angle Tarn near Patterdale, which is redeemed by its islands, rocky shoreline and remarkable panorama of the Helvellyn fells) from a lack of encircling crags and any sense of drama – is crossed on strategic-ally placed stepping stones. The turf here is springy but has been worn away in places to leave a bare peat trench leading up the steep slope opposite. For some time on this tiring climb, consola-tion is provided by the sight of what appears to be the first crinkle on the knobbly mile-long ridge of Crinkle Crags, but as height is gained even this illusion disappears when the eminence is revealed to be merely the lower and much nearer outlier of Great Knott.

Crinkle Crags can now be seen across another flat, boggy tableland. A well-marked path seeks out the best route, keeping quite close to the top of the craggy fellside overlooking Oxen-dale, and rounds Gladstone Knott to achieve the first really worth-while close-up view of the unique summit ridge of Crinkle Crags, five pinnacles of bare rock making up almost a mile of magnificent mountain scenery. The first crinkle looms ahead and to the left, and the second and third – separated by the wide fan of scree below Mickle Door – rise steeply above Great Cove, a rugged corrie containing the headwaters of Crinkle Gill but, rather surprisingly, no tarn.

After the path from Stonesty Pike comes in from the left, there is a stiff climb through boulders and then on rock to the top of the first crinkle, at 2,733ft. Down to the right are gullies falling precipitously to Great Cove, with Oxendale and the Langdale Pikes behind. On the left is the wide sweep of upper Eskdale, remote and untrodden but boasting the highest land in England as its far wall. Scafell and Scafell Pike, Esk Pike with its long western tongue advancing far into the valley, and Bowfell form a challenging quartet on the horizon. Ahead lies the best ridge walk in the Lake District, a crazily rolling course wriggling over the four remaining crinkles and the two tops of Shelter Crags before descending to Three Tarns. The undulations are more pronounced than might be expected and the path is sometimes difficult to follow, sometimes exposed and occasionally requires a little scrambling, but this is a continual delight, fascinating in detail and set in awe-inspiring rock scenery.

Beyond a miniature grassy col there is a scrambling route,

including Wainwright's 'bad step', which most walkers should in fact negotiate quite easily, to the top of the second crinkle, the highest point of **Crinkle Crags** (2,816ft). To the left the spur known as Long Top falls gently towards Eskdale; but instead of diverting along here, follow the main path past the col at Mickle Door to the next three crinkles, which are perched above impressive crags and have fine views down Langdale.

After the fifth crinkle, which has the distinction of being separately named as Gunson Knott, there is another descent (scarcely longer than those between individual crinkles) and then another climb to the twin summits of Shelter Crags, at 2,680ft. Here a major attraction is a small tarn in a hollow between the two rocky bluffs, a perfect foreground for the Scafell range and Bowfell. Descend easily over rocks and then grass to the wide and draughty col at **Three Tarns**, the scene now dominated by the overpowering bulk of Bowfell. There are four or five pools lying in hollows in the glacial debris on this ridge, and the three principal tarns are an attractive sight amongst the weathered grey boulders and close-cropped grass.

The wide and severely eroded track up the spur known as The Band, from Great Langdale to Bowfell, can be seen approaching from the right. Repairs have been carried out quite effectively where the track strikes up the fellside behind Stool End Farm, but really the whole length of the track is in the same sorry state. The answer to the problem is not at all obvious; if nothing is done the mountain will become permanently disfigured, but the only alternative seems to be an artificial surface of boards or regular stone steps, as on the Pennine Way in parts of the Peak District. The problem of erosion through over-use is equally obvious on the path up from Three Tarns to the summit of Bowfell, and it is worth considering spreading the load by dropping down to the Climber's Traverse, which undulates excitingly close to the fine crags on the Mickleden face of the mountain, and then ascending between Cambridge Crag and Bowfell Buttress. Another possibility is to find a scrambling route on the easy rocks to the right of the path, but not too close to the edge of the major crags.

The summit of **Bowfell** (2,960ft) lies well to the west of the crags, on a rocky plateau strewn with boulders of all shapes and sizes. The rugged top is entirely in keeping with the rest of this superb mountain, which has fine crags on three sides and an instantly recognisable conical outline. The view is magnificent; clockwise from Great Langdale, it features Pike of Blisco and Crinkle Crags, with the Coniston Fells between them, the full length of Eskdale to the sea, the Scafell range with the gash of Mickledore seemingly close at hand, Great Gable behind Esk Pike, the north-western fells hazily in the distance, Skiddaw and Blencathra, the long ridge of the Helvellyn fells, High Street behind the Langdale Pikes, and then the deep bowl of Langdale again.

Nail scratches on the boulders are the best guide to the cairned path leading down from Bowfell to Ore Gap, an ancient but now little used through route from Eskdale to Langstrath. The soil here is bright red in places, evidence of the vein of haematite which runs down the Eskdale side of the hause. Some iron ore was mined here in medieval times (when it was taken down Langstrath for smelting) and again in the eighteenth century, and there were even proposals for the building of an inclined railway, but nothing came of this and operations ceased because of the cost of getting the ore to the smelters.

Take the all too obvious path leading from Ore Gap to the summit of **Esk Pike** (2,903ft), which just scrapes a place among the ten highest Lakeland fells yet is so overshadowed by the magnificent mountains on either side that it was not even named until 1870 and did not feature on maps until much later. Yet it stands right at the head of upper Eskdale and its summit cairn is balanced on an excellent rock tor, although perhaps the best view is gained from the platform situated directly above the crags falling steeply down to Angle Tarn. Go left around the top of the crags from this viewpoint and pick up the well-marked path going down to Esk Hause. The final summit to be collected, Great End, is plainly visible in front of the familiar shape of Great Gable.

Esk Hause is one of the best-known passes in the Lake

Great End
from Ruddy Gill

District, and at 2,490ft is the highest in regular use. Many who claim to have used it have, however, merely crossed its northern shoulder, which carries the path between Langdale and Sty Head. The true hause separates Esk Pike and Great End and forms another pass between Eskdale and Langstrath, a journey which is much less often undertaken. The true hause is marked by a cairn, whereas the lower col has a cairn, a wind-shelter and sometimes even a signpost. The route lies west from the hause, climbing on the wide path heading for Scafell Pike as far as the col above Calf Cove, then swings right across extremely rough ground to reach the top of **Great End** (2,984ft). This is the north-eastern buttress of the long and high ridge of the Scafell range, and its superb northern cliffs fall a thousand feet from the rocky summit, with fantastic views down the gullies towards Sprinkling Tarn and, beyond, Borrowdale and the northern fells.

Direct routes from Great End towards Sty Head or Wasdale Head are made hazardous by the need to traverse the steep and craggy western slopes of the mountain. A route can be found on the western edge of the great cliffs falling north from the summit, but it is rough, stony and exposed and cannot be recommended for descent. A better way is to return to the col above Calf Cove, then turn right and descend, again very steeply on grass with some boulders, a prominent gully leading down to the source of Greta Gill. The gully should not be descended after rain or in icy conditions, when the combination of greasy rock and slippery grass is dangerous. A retreat to Esk Hause and **Sty Head**, a long but safer route, would then be preferable. Bear right, away from the gill, on easier ground lower down to join the Corridor route on its way from Scafell Pike to Sty Head. Then, where the Corridor route crosses the boulder-choked ravine of Skew Gill, turn down by the ravine and pick up the path leading from Sty Head to Wasdale Head.

This is the old path, carefully planned and well graded, which follows a zigzag course on the east bank of Spouthead Gill, then crosses the stream just above the confluence with Piers Gill. The steep walls of the narrow and dark ravine guarding the upper reaches of Piers Gill can be picked out on the left, below the stern slopes of Lingmell. Continue down the pleasant path on the banks of the stream, which has now become Lingmell Beck, to a wall which is frequently called upon to provide shelter from the wind and rain driving up across Wastwater towards Sty Head. The bulky and rather formless western slopes of Great End close the head of the valley, while to the north Great Gable rises magnificently, its lower slopes badly scarred by the newer and more tedious Sty Head path, but its crags rising unsullied and majestic above this intrusion.

Some distance beyond the wall, the direct track from Sty Head joins from the right and the increasingly wide path leads to Wasdale Head. Cross the wide footbridge spanning Gable Beck, pause to glance down the valley to Wastwater and the Screes, and then, skirting Burnthwaite Farm, keep to the lane as far as the small church and its protective yew trees. A field path on the right leads to the Wasdale Head Inn and the centre of the hamlet of **Wasdale Head** (see the Valley Route for details). Behind is Great End, an impressive reminder of an arduous but exhilarating ridge walk over five excellent fells at the heart of Lakeland.

2   GREAT GABLE
Wasdale Head to Rosthwaite (8 miles/13km)

For more than half a mile the route lies across the territory covered on the previous afternoon, past Burnthwaite Farm to the footbridge crossing Gable Beck. Then, turn up immediately to the left and begin to climb the steep south-west ridge of Great Gable. This is Gavel Neese (also ascended as far as Moses' Finger by the Valley Route in which further details but scant encouragement will be found). Although the initial stages are on turf, the angle is such that progress will be slow and laborious; later, when the surface turns to scree, it may well become almost non-existent. Eventually, a secure resting place can be found at Moses' Finger, a rock bastion in a river of loose stones, and there will be a tremendous temptation to relax and enjoy the

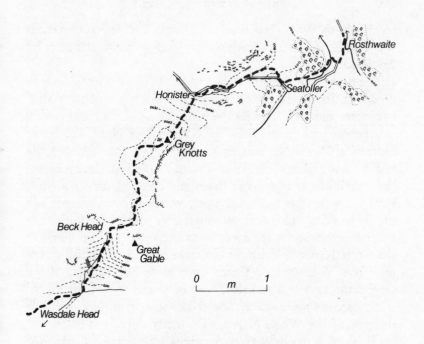

magnificent view down the length of Wasdale.

The temptation should, however, be firmly resisted for there is a great deal of hard work left before Great Gable is conquered (the consolation is that the view is even better from the Westmorland Cairn on the edge of the summit plateau). The first decision is the choice of route: all the variations are rewarding, though some are rather more challenging than others. Without this large choice of routes the Gable, over-populated as it so frequently is, would be in a desperate condition. As it is, many of the paths are deeply cut into the fellside, and rivers of scree have been formed on parts of the most popular routes.

The choice from Moses' Finger is comparatively simple: straight up, leading to a difficult scramble over White Napes, or right, along the Gable Traverse and then up to the summit by a variety of possible ways. (Just to complicate matters, it is also possible to take the path leading left from just below Moses' Finger – the Valley Route goes this way – to Beck Head, and then up alongside Gable Crag by a steep and exciting route over

rocks.) Both White Napes and the Gable Traverse are excellent
ways to the top, with superb scenery close at hand, and both are
described.

The route from Moses' Finger to the White Napes is never in
doubt. It lies up the unremittingly steep shoulder of the Gable,
over scree and rock, and just below the base of the rocks crosses
the traverse path from Little Hell Gate to Beck Head. The lower
buttress of White Napes is set at an invitingly comfortable angle
and there is a wide choice of easy routes, although since much of
the scrambling is over loose flakes and boulders care is needed.
Higher up there is a delicate arête, which is much steeper and
should be skirted to its left, although after a while the angle eases
and the arête can be regained, with excellent close-up views of
the Great Napes to the right, to make a satisfying finish to the
scramble. Westmorland Crags now lie to the right, and the
second route, described below, can be joined at their base.

This second route, to the South Traverse, continues almost to
the base of the White Napes, then heads right, just below the
crags, until it meets a river of scree, aptly named Little Hell
Gate. This is one of the two scree channels which define the
limits of the Great Napes, arguably the finest series of crags in
the Lake District. Immediately to the right of the scree is the
Sphinx Ridge, and this is followed by Arrowhead Ridge, Eagle's
Nest Ridge, Needle Ridge (with Napes Needle towards its base)
and Tophet Bastion. The five ridges are divided by sharp, deeply
riven gullies, and at the far end is the steep scree run of Great
Hell Gate. The Great Napes tapers to a grass platform above the
highest crags of its constituent ridges, and above this platform
the Westmorland Crags defend the summit of the mountain.

It is perfectly possible to use Little Hell Gate as a route to the
summit, climbing the shifting stairway of scree past the Sphinx
Rock to the top of the Napes and then skirting Westmorland
Crags to get to the top of Great Gable. Such a route would miss
the chief glory of the South Traverse, however, which is its
unrivalled views of the striking rock scenery of the Napes ridges.
So press on across Little Hell Gate and pick up the South
Traverse below Sphinx Ridge, notable for the protruding

buttress known as the Sphinx Rock or Cat Rock after its appearance from two vantage points.

Generally, the traverse keeps some distance below the base of the crags under Arrowhead Ridge and Eagle's Nest Ridge, although it is possible to scramble up below the latter to see at closer quarters the dark cleft of Needle Gully separating the steep lower rocks of Eagle's Nest Ridge from Needle Ridge, its bulkier crags serving to emphasise the extraordinary pinnacle of Napes Needle in the lower reaches of the ridge. The Needle was first climbed in 1886 by W. P. Haskett-Smith, who occupies a legendary position in accounts of early British rock climbing, yet it pales into insignificance when seen in the context of the Great Napes as a whole. Only the romance associated with its place in rock-climbing history, and the 'picture postcard' nature of its location astride the soaring Needle Ridge, justify its status as one of the best-known mountain features in Britain.

Beyond Needle Ridge, the South Traverse maintains a height of about two thousand feet as it weaves between rock buttresses at the base of Tophet Bastion, which as its name implies is an enormous and steeply inclined buttress forming the eastern wall of the Great Napes and projecting forward from the mountain as if to emphasise the sheer volume of rock encompassed within this astonishing array of crags. Where the South Traverse begins to lose height, leave it and begin to climb the reddish screes of Great Hell Gate.

There is no easy way to ascend the steep, loose scree funnelling between Tophet Bastion and the lesser crags to the east, although it may be worth keeping close to the left edge of the scree shoot in places in the search for a firmer footing. Towards the top, Hell Gate Pillar provides a welcome island of certainty in the sea of shifting stones, and above here the slope eases and the grassy ridge connecting the Great Napes to Westmorland Crags can quickly be gained. Bypass the crags on the left and then bear right to reach the Westmorland cairn on the edge of the summit plateau.

Built by the Westmorland brothers in 1876, the cairn is situated immediately above the precipitous crags and therefore has virtually an aerial view of Wasdale, with the network of stone-walled fields around Wasdale Head, the majestic fells of Scafell and its neighbours, and the brooding lake of Wastwater framed by the Screes, together comprising a scene which sums up the extraordinary appeal of the Lake District. And a hundred yards or so away across the boulder field is the summit of **Great Gable** (2,949ft), another of the special places in the Lake District and, as a tablet affixed to a boulder near the cairn indicates, the site of the Fell and Rock Climbing Club's war memorial. A remarkable mountain, defended by tremendous rock precipices yet accessible by a number of excellent walker's routes, Great Gable has been described by Harry Griffin as 'the quintessential fell' and, not surprisingly, it provides the centrepiece for the Lake District National Park's emblem.

The second objective of the day is Green Gable, which is inferior not only in stature but also in character to Great Gable. Take the obvious and eroded path slanting down over boulders above Gable Crag to the aptly named Windy Gap but, where most of the traffic turns right down Aaron Slack, keep on along the ridge, with fine views to the left encompassing the head of Ennerdale and the High Stile group of fells. The ridge leads quickly to the quite sharply defined summit of **Green Gable** (2,603ft), an excellent viewpoint for the astonishingly intricate rock walls and gullies of Gable Crag. Few people linger on this subsidiary summit, and the fine grouping of the fells crowding around Buttermere and Crummock Water often passes unseen.

Continue north from Green Gable, initially in the direction of Brandreth, but at a junction of paths fork right down to a col at the head of Gillercomb, a superb hanging valley backed by the dark wall of Raven Crag, plunging 600ft from the ridge of Brandreth to the flat, marshy floor of the corrie basin. The summit of **Base Brown** (2,120ft) lies north-east of the col, across a broad and gently inclined tableland of grass. Around the highest point a few outcrops of rock enliven the scene, but these and the large summit cairn serve only to emphasise the change in scenery from the rock mountain of Great Gable to the sheepwalk of Base Brown.

Yet Base Brown's summit scarcely does justice to the fell as a whole, as can be seen when the narrowing north-east ridge is taken on the way to Seathwaite. The path weaves between rock outcrops in places and the crags on either side of the ridge lend an air of grandeur to the scene. Eventually the ridge itself peters out in a tumbling mass of low crags, and some care is needed in edging down past the Hanging Stone, a small perched boulder named on maps but really rather unexciting, to the valley of Sour Milk Gill. This is the stream which looks so attractive from Seathwaite when in spate, but the over-used path down alongside its south bank is somewhat trying in places over steep and rough terrain. Below the cascades, cross the river Derwent on a war memorial footbridge to reach the hamlet of Seathwaite.

Infamous as the wettest inhabited place in England, with an annual rainfall of around one-hundred-and-fifty inches, **Seathwaite** is also important as the start of the much-trodden route over Sty Head to Wasdale. This track probably dates from the seventeenth century and was an important packhorse route; indeed at that time it was metalled and slightly raised above the flood plain of the Derwent between Seathwaite and Stockley Bridge. Since the end of the packhorse era it has gradually deteriorated, and the combined effects of walkers and the 1966 floods, which destroyed Stockley Bridge and brought down a sea of boulders to choke the stream bed and gouge out the path, have just about destroyed all evidence of its former importance.

Between Stockley Bridge and Seathwaite the Sty Head path cuts through a series of moraines. This hummocky glacial drift, composed of clay, gravel and rounded boulders, probably dates from the end of the Ice Age and is only one of a series of glacial features in this upper section of Borrowdale. Between Seathwaite and Seatoller the flat valley floor was once a lake, and south of Thornythwaite Farm a recessional end moraine (a deposit left by the ice as it retreated when the climate improved) can be picked out as a low ridge running across the valley floor.

The most obvious route northwards from Seathwaite lies along the road to **Seatoller**, but this is extremely congested in summer and a far better way lies along the base of Thorny-

Glaramara, Derwentwater
and Skiddaw

thwaite Fell, the north-western spur of Glaramara. Take the field
path east of the road and follow Black Sike, a minor tributary of
the Derwent, alongside the intake wall. Across the valley the
Borrowdale Yews, the 'fraternal four' immortalised by Wordsworth, survive doggedly. They were damaged by a gale in 1883
and only three remain, in a fairly decrepit condition.

Above the yews is the site of the graphite mine which gave rise
to the Keswick pencil industry. With some difficulty the remains
of the enterprise can be discovered on the fellside of Grey Knotts:
the cobbled pony track from Seathwaite, the levels and shafts
(now in a highly dangerous condition) and the dilapidated mine
buildings. By 1600 the graphite was being used for making
pencils in Keswick, and was also used for dyeing sheep, casting
round-shot and cannon balls, and even medicinally as a cure for
colic and distemper.

The deposits became so valuable that the mine was guarded
day and night, and the miners were stripped and searched when
leaving the workings. One single deposit of thirty tons
discovered in 1803 was worth an incredible £100,000. It is hardly
surprising that intrigue and robbery were common (much of it

apparently organised in the bars of The George Hotel in Keswick) and the graphite was accompanied by armed guards as far as Kendal. Despite this, a good deal was spirited away along Moses' Trod and down into Wasdale. Finally, as alternative supplies were brought in from abroad the price of graphite dropped and the mine fell into disuse in the late nineteenth century.

The fell path alongside Black Sike eventually joins the farm road just to the east of Thornythwaite Farm, and then follows this to the banks of the River Derwent and alongside the river to the main road at Mountain View cottages. **Rosthwaite** lies three-quarters of a mile along the road, although one of two variations can be used to reduce the amount of road walking. One carries on along the river bank, crosses the river on Folly Bridge and takes the path through Johnny Wood used by the Valley Route. The other turns right along the valley road, then takes the footpath on the right at Burthwaite Bridge and visits the hamlet of Borrowdale. A chapel-of-ease was constructed here in 1687, but in less than a hundred years was in disrepair, and the present whitewashed chapel, with its simple bell-cote, dates mostly from 1825, when rebuilding cost £300, and a restoration in 1873. From the chapel the lane from Stonethwaite can be followed to the main road which leads straight to Rosthwaite.

3. GLARAMARA AND THE LANGDALE PIKES
Rosthwaite to Great Langdale (13 miles/21km)

The first half mile of this walk is a tedious grind; the rest, with the possible exception of the trudge across Martcrag Moor, is a magnificent walk in outstandingly attractive mountain country, and should be high on the list of every walker's priorities. It starts, however, with the road walk from Rosthwaite to Mountain View. Opposite the cottages, take the lane leading to Thornythwaite, but then quickly turn left beyond the first field wall and, with the scenery improving all the time, walk through the wood to the course of Comb Gill. Beyond the sawmill, tracks

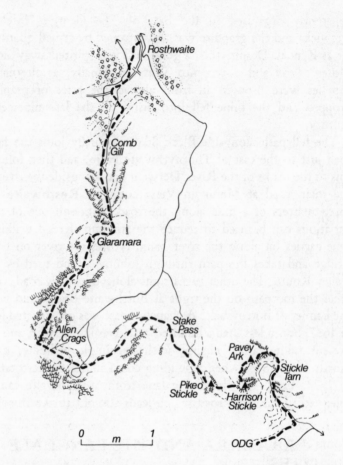

Comb Gill

Rosthwaite

Glaramara

Allen
Crags

Stake
Pass

Pavey
Ark

Pike o'
Stickle

Stickle
Tarn

Harrison
Stickle

0   m   1

ODG

rise on either side of the stream, but they eventually converge on
the west bank.

Comb Gill is a superb example of a hanging valley, and has
the added attraction of solemn crags on either flank. Yet it is rare
for the path to be overcrowded, and the excellent natural route
up by the side of the gill to the skyline at Comb Door and then
to the top of Glaramara along the ridge is an exciting way to a
fine viewpoint. After a marshy mid-section, the crags begin to
rise on either side of the valley, with Raven Crag to the right
and Dove's Nest Crag closing in on the left. Dove's Nest Crag is
the more famous, partly because a section of the rock face

slumped forward many centuries ago to leave a series of caves between the landslip and the heart of the crag. More recently there have been rockfalls, and since 1979 warning notices have directed explorers away from the caves, which previously offered an unusual torchlight route to the ridge. Now, in their present highly dangerous state, they should be avoided.

Raven Crag, on the other side of the valley, is of more interest to rock climbers than walkers, but its strikingly clean lines are enough to extract admiration from anyone passing beneath its massive face. The dark cliff torn apart by deep, long gullies is a perfect introduction to the character of the steep, stony and rough upper section of Comb Gill. There is a difficult scramblers' route up the bed of the gill itself, but where this becomes a ravine the way forward is anything but obvious and escape can be hazardous. Fell walkers will probably prefer to keep to the right of the ravine, over bouldery but comparatively easy territory, with glimpses of the waterfalls on the way to the vividly defined gash of Comb Door, on the ridge between Cam Crag and Glaramara.

The substantial and elegant summit cairn of **Glaramara** (2,560ft) is easily if steeply gained from Comb Door, with a reward of spectacular views in almost every direction. Glaramara is Old Norse for 'the shieling [or shepherd's hut] at the head of the ravine', and the finest prospect of all is that northwards along Comb Gill and over Derwentwater to the noble heights of Skiddaw and Blencathra. Yet this superb panorama by no means exhausts the potential of Glaramara as a platform for viewing the surrounding fells. Although Scafell and Scafell Pike are obscured by the intervening heights of Great End and Ill Crag, Great Gable, a constant companion for the next stage of the walk, is especially prominent, and the fells around Grasmoor are seen in perfect perspective.

Leave Glaramara, pausing only to survey the site of a stone axe factory just below the summit to the north, by taking the obvious footpath heading over the rocky ridge in the direction of Allen Crags. This is a magnificent ridge walk over broken and fascinating terrain, enhanced by a series of picturesque little tarns. Follow the line of cairns over rough and undulating ground to a slight depression which is often boggy, then past Lincomb Tarn, a superb ridge tarn in a rocky basin, and High House Tarn, the largest of the pools and the only one named on the map. The path passes another two or three small tarns and reaches Allen Crags up a simple grassy slope.

Allen Crags (2,572ft) lies immediately north of Esk Hause, a busy walkers' crossroads, yet its summit is rarely visited except as an afterthought by walkers bound for Glaramara. In some ways this neglect is understandable, since the summit is merely a shapeless hump with a severe outbreak of cairns. Yet this is a fell which, as a result of its location on a spur running north from Great End, is intimately connected with some of the finest mountain scenery in the Lake District. The massive dark, splintered north wall of Great End itself blocks the southern horizon, while round to the west, across the attractive high-level pool of Sprinkling Tarn, lies Great Gable. The crags adorning the Wasdale face of this remarkable mountain can readily be identified, and beyond them are Red Pike, Pillar and the other fells of the Mosedale Horseshoe.

A path picks its way down the southern slopes of Allen Crags to meet the major track running from Sty Head to Great Langdale at the substantial wind-shelter just north-east of and below Esk Hause. Turn left along this path and follow it for about half a mile to Angle Tarn, an exquisite corrie tarn cradled by Hanging Knotts, the stern northern buttress of Bowfell. Trapped on its shelf between the stepped cliffs to the south and the steady drop down into Langstrath to the north, Angle Tarn has the reputation of being dark and unfriendly, and rarely visited by the sun. Yet it is one of the most hauntingly attractive of the corrie tarns, and a popular spot for picnics and casual camp sites.

Continue past the tarn on the Langdale path, but when this begins to lose height quickly at the head of Rossett Gill contour round to the left to visit the top of another much-maligned fell, Rossett Pike (2,106ft). Strictly speaking this is an outlying spur of Bowfell, but it has its own graceful and sharply defined summit cone, and from near here there is probably the best view

The Langdale Pikes
and Allen Crags

of the glacial trough of Mickleden, lying between the mountain wall continuing to the Langdale Pikes on the left, and on the right The Band, the eastern spur of Bowfell. Rossett Pike is also a highly effective viewpoint for the crags of Bowfell, from the oblique slab of Flat Crags round to Bowfell Buttress, serrated and precipitous.

North-east from Rossett Pike a path strikes across a particularly stony ridge over Buck Pike to Littlegill Head, and then curves round to the right of the top rocks of Lining Crag, the only notable feature amidst the grassy moorland forming the Langstrath side of Rossett Pike. The immediate objective is the prominent cairn marking the marshy summit of **Stake Pass** (1,576ft), so called because the way across the wide flat moorland was originally marked by a series of stakes. On either side, hummocky moraine litters the heads of minor valleys, and in front stretches the wide, wet and featureless Martcrag Moor. Only the remarkable sight of the Langdale Pikes, and in particular Pike o' Stickle, rising spectacularly above the boggy moorland, lifts the spirits at this point.

This dreary moorland was, however, the place where the first evidence of stone axes was discovered. In the 1920s Professor D. M. S. Watson climbed up to the plateau and collected several rough axe heads from an erosion channel in the dark brown peat. He came to the conclusion that the raw material was normally loose scree, although occasionally the slate had been split away from larger boulders. It was not until 1947 that the much more widely known site on the higher scree slopes of Pike o' Stickle was discovered.

The route onwards from the top of Stake Pass lies across the peat wastes to the firmer footing at the edge of the steep slopes overlooking Mickleden. A cairn here indicates a fine view of Bowfell across Rossett Gill. Beyond the marshy head of Troughton Beck, there is a steady but comparatively easy climb, latterly over awkward boulders, to the top of **Pike o' Stickle** (2,323ft). The ascent is naturally more dramatic direct from Great Langdale, with the cliffs and scree soaring above the valley, but even from this less familiar line of attack the last few feet call for some scrambling over easy rocks. The area around the summit cairn is, however, surprisingly grassy. The view downwards some two thousand feet into Langdale is impressive and somewhat daunting, but in other directions, with the exception of the head of Mickleden, it is a little disappointing.

Harrison Stickle, the highest of the Langdale Pikes, is the next top to be visited and it is easily gained across the marshy intervening ground of Harrison Combe. The sluggish stream which has its source here becomes Dungeon Ghyll, a stream whose lower course is a series of plunging cascades, desperate ravines and spectacular waterfalls. The summit ridge of **Harrison Stickle** (2,403ft) is defended by crags on three sides and has an appropriately rocky appearance. Various vantage points on the little ridge command the best views of particular features, but the overall effect is stunning. A broad sweep of Windermere dominates the scene to the south-east, while Crinkle Crags and Bowfell form a challenging south-westerly horizon, and the dome of Great Gable overshadows its neighbours in the west. The distant northern fells are excellently grouped, but the desolate plateau in the foreground detracts from this picture. The rugged cliff of Pavey Ark to the left of the deep hollow containing Stickle Tarn steals the show to the north-east.

Pavey Ark is also the next destination, and the half-mile walk to its summit is highly entertaining. Head north from Harrison Stickle, descending gradually over excellent rocks to meet a wide path coming up from Stickle Tarn. Leave this on the left and take a direct route to the summit of **Pavey Ark** (2,288ft), again mostly over rocks, though since there is no exposure and the gradients are very gentle this can hardly be called scrambling. During the approach, Pavey Ark appears as a pleasantly rounded dome consisting almost entirely of little rock slabs interspersed with boulders, and around the summit this is certainly true. Even more interesting are the fantastic views down the gully exits and of the pinnacles rising from the magnificent cliff south of the summit, a cliff which is the back wall of Stickle Tarn's corrie.

One of the gully exits, to the south-east of the summit cairn, forms the highest point of Jack's Rake, the adventurous scrambler's way down to Stickle Tarn, but certainly not recommended to novices or to those uncertain of their ability to descend steep rock. In rain or snow the rake should be left to the experts, but it is a superb direct route and, shielded in part by a natural rock parapet, leaves the walker with curiously little sense of exposure. The top section lies over comparatively easy rocks into Great Gully; then, slightly lower down the gully, there is a left turn into the rake proper, which at this point consists of a rock groove. The rake continues below precipitous cliffs, on steep grass and then awkward and slightly exposed rocks, to reach the foot of the East Buttress, and a footpath leading round Stickle Tarn.

Undoubtedly the descent of Jack's Rake is one of the most difficult bits of scrambling described in this book, and it is getting slightly more difficult with the passage of time and feet, with the inevitable severe erosion which has transformed the surface into dangerously loose rock in places. Consequently many will think it wiser to seek an easier way down. The North Rake (a name improvised by Wainwright) fits the bill admirably. Leave the summit cairn to the north, passing a small pool and crossing a drystone wall, then swing round to the right to pick up a cairned path. This path appears to be heading straight for the crags but actually leads to a grassy rake between the main wall of Pavey Ark and its more broken northern crags. Follow the rake down quite steeply to reach Bright Beck, the main feeder of Stickle Tarn, and keep to its east bank as far as the tarn.

Stickle Tarn, unusual amongst corrie tarns in that it faces south, is in all other respects a fine example of the species. It is dominated by the huge black wall of Pavey Ark – the line of Jack's Rake as it rises diagonally across the cliff from right to left is distinct and inviting – and lies at the lip of a rock step down which Mill Gill plunges steeply into Great Langdale. Yet the tarn, in its present state, is artificial. It was much enlarged in the nineteenth century to provide a water supply for the old gunpowder works at Elterwater and the dam is still intact.

There is now only a mile left before the Heart of Lakeland route reaches Great Langdale, but the direct descent on either side of Mill Gill (wrongly called Stickle Gill on some maps) is likely to be extremely crowded and on paths which are being virtually demolished by the passage of feet. This is one of the key areas in the Lake District where a solution has to be found to the problems of visitor pressure, but so far little success has been achieved. However, other lines of descent can be picked out, and are far pleasanter if a little longer. The attractive path passing between Pike Howe and Harrison Stickle is one possibility, and there are others to the east.

The Langdale Pikes
from New Dungeon Ghyll

All the routes converge on the New Dungeon Ghyll Hotel, which like the Old Dungeon Ghyll half a mile further up the valley was a farm in the medieval period. The ODG can be quickly and enjoyably reached by taking the track running at the base of the fells, below Dungeon Ghyll Force (which can be reached by a short detour over the intervening spur) and Raven Crag. At one time this was the main road up the valley from Chapel Stile to Middlefell Place and Mickleden, but it is now a level green track. Turn off left to reach the Climber's Bar of the ODG, an appropriate place to end a three-day excursion which has included the rocky traverse of the Crinkle Crags ridge, a scrambling route to the top of Great Gable and (perhaps) a difficult but exhilarating descent of Jack's Rake on Pavey Ark, three examples of the magnificent rewards awaiting walkers who venture into the Heart of Lakeland.

BIBLIOGRAPHY

An astonishing number of books has been written on the Lake District and various facets of its history, topography and culture, but relatively few of them are of interest to fell walkers. In the following notes I have tried to select those that I have found useful or enjoyable or, preferably, both.

Most of the older topographical volumes can be passed over with few qualms, since they are mostly outdated and often virtually unreadable. The shining exception is William Wordsworth's *Guide to the Lakes* (originally published as such in 1835; 5th edition, with an introduction by E. de Selincourt, Oxford University Press, 1977), which is a perceptive and sympathetic survey. The modern classic is A. Wainwright's *A Pictorial Guide to the Lakeland Fells* (Westmorland Gazette, 1955–66), which comprises seven attractive and still highly prized volumes giving detailed descriptions of every fell.

Two complementary books which between them cover the mountains of the area pretty well are Walt Unsworth's *The High Fells of Lakeland* (Robert Hale, 1972), a highly entertaining guide with a chapter devoted to each of the main groups of fells, and Frank Goddard's *Foothills of the Fells* (Robert Hale, 1981), a useful book, if a little anecdotal in places. *Scrambles in the Lake District*, by Brian Evans (Cicerone Press, 1982), is a particularly welcome addition to fell walking literature since it describes a number of exciting routes to Lakeland summits. One of the books by the most prolific modern writer on the area, A. H. Griffin, also qualifies for inclusion in this brief survey: *Freeman of the Hills* (Robert Hale, 1978) is a superb character study of the Lakeland Twothousanders. At a generally lower altitude, Hunter Davies' *A Walk Around the Lakes* (Weidenfeld & Nicholson, 1979) is readable and contains useful information.

Wayside oak, Cat Bells

A couple of books dealing with more general walking topics should also be mentioned. *Across Northern Hills*, by Geoffrey Berry (Westmorland Gazette, 1975) has a brief chapter on the Roman Way, and Alan Mattingly's *Walking in the National Parks* (David & Charles, 1980) includes a chapter on the Lake District.

Two academic books are so outstandingly useful in appreciating the evolution of the region's landscape that they deserve inclusion in this brief list. *The Lake District*, by Roy Millward and Adrian Robinson (Eyre Methuen, 1974) is essential reading for its carefully researched chronological presentation, and *The Lake District: a Landscape History*, by W. H. Pearsall and Winifred Pennington (Collins, 1973), though grounded in natural history, is extremely informative. The Countryside Commission's *Lake District* National Park guide (HMSO, 1975) is less weighty but still packed with interesting information.

Useful publications dealing with more specialised subjects include *Real Ale in Cumbria* (Campaign for Real Ale, 1982), Wayne Davies' *The Ravenglass and Eskdale Railway* (David & Charles, 1981), *Archaeological Sites of the Lake District* by T. Clare (Moorland Publishing, 1981) and the beautifully illustrated tribute to the Lake District's most dramatically attractive valley, *Wasdale: a Celebration in Words and Pictures*, by Ruth Eversley (Michael Moon, 1981).

Grisedale

INDEX

Addacomb Hole, 47, 48
Allen Crags, 208
Ambleside, 17, 115, 116–17
Angle Tarn (Bowfell), 195, 208
Angle Tarn (Patterdale), 70, 192
Applethwaite, 54

Bakestall, 88
Bannerdale Crags, 97
Base Brown, 202–3
Bassenthwaite, 16, 84–5
Bassenthwaite Lake, 83, 84, 86, 89
Beck Head, 161–2
Binsey, 83, 87
Black Sail Hut, 41
Blea Water, 111, 186
Bleaberry Tarn, 43, 44, 45, 144
Blease Fell, 59, 90
Blencathra, 27, 57–8, 91, 92–6, 148
Blue Gill, 111
Boat How, 154
Boot, 16, 18, 37, 128, 153–4
Boredale Hause, 69
Borrowdale, 17, 51, 139, 166, 169, 205
Bowfell, 194–5, 208
Bowscale Fell, 97
Bowscale Tarn, 79, 97–8
Braithwaite, 149–50
Brandreth, 163, 202
Branstree, 185
Brigham, 23, 52, 64, 138
Brim Fell, 26
Brocavum, 100
Brotherilkeld, 16, 29–30, 127
Brougham, 17, 100–1
Burnmoor, 37, 154–5
Burnmoor Tarn, 155–6
Burnthwaite, 156, 161, 198

Buttermere, 18, 43, 45–6, 141, 144, 164
Buttermere Moss, 143

Campbell, Sir Donald, 23
Carrock Fell, 77, 78–9
Carrock Mine, 81
Catbells, 51, 138–9
Causey Pike, 46, 49
Clough Head, 61, 91
Cockermouth, 17, 147
Cockley Beck, 28, 124
Coledale, 48, 146, 149
Coleridge, Samuel Taylor, 86–7
Colwith Force, 118–20
Comb Gill, 206–7
Coniston, 16, 17, 23
Coniston Water, 17, 23, 26
Copperheap Bay, 137–8
Crinkle Crags, 193–4
Crummock Water, 44–5, 47, 146

Dale Head, 140–1
Dalegarth Force, 129
Dash Falls, 83, 86–7
Davies, Hunter, 215
Dead Crags, 83, 86, 87
Deer Bields, 171
Derwentwater, 17, 49, 57, 89, 137
Dollywaggon Pike, 177
Dove Cottage, 173
Dove's Nest Crag, 206–7
Dow Crag, 25–6
Driggith Mine, 79
Duddon, River, 28, 123–4
Dunmail Raise, 23, 172, 175

Eagle Crag, 168
Eamont Bridge, 102

Eel Crag, 48, 147, 148
Ennerdale, 21, 39ff, 202
Ennerdale Water, 41
Eskdale, 28, 29ff, 125ff, 152–3, 193
Eskdale Green, 130
Esk Hause, 30, 195–6, 208
Esk Pike, 195
Evans, Brian, 215

Fairfield, 177
Far Easedale, 170
Fell Foot, 121–2
Forestry Commission, 30, 41, 149
Foule Crag, 58, 96
Fountains Abbey, 168
Froswick, 74, 111
Furness Abbey, 30, 32, 118, 120

Galava, 28, 116–17
Garburn Road, 75, 113
Gategill, 59, 93
Gatescarth Pass, 184, 185
Gavel Neese, 160–1, 198
Glannaventa, 28, 133
Glaramara, 167, 207
Glenderamackin, River, 57, 77, 94, 96–7
Glenridding, 64, 67–8, 181
Goats Water, 25, 26
Goddard, Frank, 215
Grasmere, 17, 172–3
Grasmoor, 43, 46, 47, 145–6
Great Carrs, 27
Great Cockup, 83
Great Crosthwaite, 51
Great Dodd, 62
Great End, 197, 208
Great Gable, 11, 41, 42, 160–1, 198ff, 208
Great Hell Gate, 200–1
Great Langdale, 17, 18, 118, 191, 210, 212
Great Lingy Hill, 81
Great Moss, 32
Great Napes, 161, 200
Great Sca Fell, 82
Green Gable, 163, 202
Greenside Mine, 50, 64, 67
Greenup Edge, 169–70

Grey Crag, 184–5
Grey Friar, 28
Grey Knotts, 163, 204
Griffin, Harry, 13, 65, 92, 215
Grisedale, 176ff
Grisedale Pike, 148

Hall's Fell, 59, 92–4
Hardknott Castle, see Mediobogdum
Hardknott Pass, 28, 29, 120
Harrison Stickle, 210–11
Harter Fell (Eskdale), 26, 28, 127
Harter Fell (Mardale), 187
Haweswater, 73, 110, 184, 185–6
Hayeswater, 71, 110
Haystacks, 42
Helm Crag, 171, 173, 175
Helvellyn, 60, 65–6, 94, 172, 177
High Crag, 43
High Pike, 80
High Spy, 140
High Stile, 43
High Street, 70, 73, 110–11, 187
Hobcarton Crag, 146–7, 148
Honister, 140, 160, 163–4
Hopegill Head, 146–7
Howtown, 16, 106–7

Ill Bell, 74, 112

Jack's Rake, 211–12
Johnny Wood, 165–6

Kentmere, 18, 74, 111, 182, 189
Kentmere Reservoir, 74, 183, 188
Keppelcove Tarn, 64, 67
Keswick, 16, 17, 52–3, 137, 139, 151, 205
Kinn, 150
Knott, 82

Lake District Weather Service, 20
Langstrath, 168, 195
Lanty Slee, 120
Lingcove Bridge, 32–3
Lingholm, 51, 137
Little Hell Gate, 200
Little Langdale, 118, 121

Little Narrowcove, 33
Loadpot Hill, 105, 107
Long Stile, 73, 110, 187
Longsleddale, 184
Lonscale Fell, 56, 89
Looking Stead, 41
Lord's Rake, 36
Low Hartsop, 71
Lowther House, 105–6

Maiden Moor, 140
Mardale, 17, 73
Mardale Green, 185–6
Mardale Ill Bell, 187
Martindale, 72, 106–7
Mayburgh, 103
Meal Fell, 82
Mediobogdum, 29, 124–5
Mickleden, 192, 209
Mickledore, 33, 34, 36
Miterdale, 130, 154
Moor Divock, 104
Mosedale (near Mungrisdale), 78
Mosedale (Wasdale), 37, 156, 159
Moses' Finger, 198
Moses' Trod, 160, 162–3, 205
Muncaster Castle, 130, 132
Muncaster Fell, 130–1
Mungrisdale, 17, 77, 98–9

Nan Bield Pass, 187
Napes Needle, 31, 201
Narrow Edge, 95–6
National Trust, 41, 52, 75, 113, 117,
     139, 190
Newlands, 50, 52, 140–1, 144

Old Corpse Road, 37, 154
Old Dungeon Ghyll Hotel, 190, 214
Old Man of Coniston, 23, 24, 26
Ore Gap, 168, 195
Orthwaite, 83

Patterdale, 18, 68–9, 180
Pavey Ark, 211
Pen, 33
Penny Hill, 127

Penrith, 17, 100
Pike o' Stickle, 34, 210
Pike of Blisco, 192
Pillar, 40
Pillar Rock, 25, 40–1, 42
Portinscale, 51, 151
Potter, Beatrix, 113

Raise, 64
Rampsgill Head, 109
Rannerdale, 46, 145
Ravenglass, 17, 120, 134–5
Ravenglass & Eskdale railway, 18, 130,
     134, 152–3
Red Pike (Buttermere), 43–4
Red Pike (Wasdale), 39
Red Tarn (Helvellyn), 65–6
Red Tarn (Pike of Blisco), 192
Rest Dodd, 71
Riggindale, 73, 110, 186
Ritson, Will, 156–8
Robinson, 143
Robinson's Cairn, 40
Rossett Pike, 208
Rosthwaite, 166, 205
Rushbearing, 117, 173
Ruskin, John, 23, 95

Sadgill, 184
Sail, 48
Scafell, 34, 35–6, 154, 155
Scafell Crag, 25, 35, 36
Scafell Pike, 33, 34, 35, 197
Scales Tarn, 58, 96
Scar Crags, 48
Scarth Gap, 41
Scoat Fell, 39
Scott, Sir Walter, 62
Seat Sandal, 176
Seathwaite, 52, 203
Seatoller, 21, 165, 203
Sharp Edge, 58, 96
Shipman Knotts, 189
Skelwith Force, 118
Skiddaw, 53–4, 56, 85, 88
Skiddaw Forest, 56, 88
Skiddaw House, 56, 79, 86, 87, 90
Skiddaw Little Man, 55, 88–9

Slater Bridge, 120
Small Water, 187
Society for the Mines Royal, 140
Southey, Robert, 43, 53
Stair, 48, 50
Stake Pass, 210
Statesman farms, 30, 51, 71, 76
Steeple, 39
Stickle Tarn, 211–12
Sticks Pass, 50, 63, 67
Stone Age axe factories, 34, 210
Stonethwaite, 167
Stonycroft, 50, 64, 141
Striding Edge, 58, 65, 178
Sty Head, 159, 197, 203
Stybarrow Dodd, 63
Swirl How, 27
Swirral Edge, 65, 66

Tarn Crag, 185
The Band, 194, 209
The Knott, 72
Thirlmere, 62
Thornthwaite Crag, 74, 111, 113
Three Shire Stone, 123
Three Tarns, 194
Threlkeld, 17, 56, 59, 86, 91
Threlkeld Knotts settlement, 61, 94
Tirril, 103
Town End, 75
Troutbeck, 17, 75–6, 114–15

Trusmadoor, 83

Ullswater, 17, 18, 68–9, 104, 107,
    180–1
Unsworth, Walt, 155, 215

Wainwright, A., 26, 89, 160, 212, 215
Walls Castle, 133–4
Walna Scar Road, 24
Wandope, 47
Wansfell Pike, 115
Wasdale, 17, 156, 217
Wasdale Head, 17, 37, 154, 156ff, 198,
    202
Wastwater, 37, 156, 202
Watson's Dodd, 62
Westmorland Cairn, 201–2
Wether Hill, 108
Wetherlam, 120, 121
Whillan Beck, 154
White Napes, 161, 200
Whiteless Pike, 46, 145
Whiteside, 64
Windermere, 17, 74, 76, 115, 211
Wordsworth, William, 37, 60, 69, 71,
    98, 172–3, 215
Wrynose Pass, 28, 120, 121, 123, 192

Yanwath, 103
Yewbarrow, 38, 155, 159
Yoke, 74, 113